CONTENTS

PREFACE

This present volume completes the studies in the Book of Acts which began with the publication of *Birth of the Body,* followed shortly by *Growth of the Body.*

Upon reading this third volume some may object that it does not relate to the theme of the Body of Christ as the first two volumes did. It is true that this last section of Acts focuses almost exclusively upon the trials and travels of the Apostle Paul, and very little mention is made of other members of the Body. Some may feel, therefore, that the title *Triumphs of the Body* is not appropriate.

The point is well-taken, though it does not seem to me of any great significance, especially in view of Paul's declaration that he and the other apostles served as a pattern for other believers. His trials would be their trials, and his triumphs would be their triumphs as well. "Be imitators of me, even as I am of Christ."

I have pointed out in this volume that the Book of Acts is unfinished, ending abruptly with Paul's first visit to Rome. This strongly implies that the Book is still being written, for each century unfolds new chapters in the story of Christ's Body on earth. Surely, therefore, the record of Paul's trials and triumphs provides a vivid and helpful example of the means by which we may prove to be more than conquerors in the trials of the Body today as well as rejoice with Paul in the TRIUMPHS.

—Ray C. Stedman

CHAPTER ONE

PAUL'S MISTAKE

Acts 21:1-26

The story of the last section of the Book of Acts is the story of Paul as a prisoner. Never before had the great apostle been locked up for more than a few days. Yet here in these last chapters we find Paul languishing for two years in the prison at Caesarea, and for three years (most scholars feel) as a prisoner in Rome. I have become convinced, however, that Paul need never have gone to Rome as a prisoner. The whole long agony of chains was totally unnecessary.

I know that the Lord Jesus, when he first called to Paul on the Damascus road, said that he was to suffer great things—but not necessarily as a prisoner. That prediction had been amply fulfilled in the hardships he had undergone in his journeys around the Roman empire. Paul had been thrown in jail from time to time, but never for very long.

I know also that the Lord Jesus said that Paul would give his testimony before kings, and I know it was the fact that he was a prisoner which finally brought him into royal courts. But again, it was not necessary that he come before kings in chains. A little later in this account the apostle himself, standing before King Agrippa, says, "I would that everyone in this room might be like I—except for these chains.'' That seems to be Paul's recognition that the chains were not a necessary part of the process.

I know, further, that it was from this prison experience that Paul wrote some of the finest letters we have. And yet the greatest letter from his pen, the letter to the Romans, was not written in prison at all. The prison letters—Colossians, Ephesians, Philippians, Philemon, and others— are evidence of the salvaging grace of God, which takes even a man's mistakes and uses them for blessing and to advance God's cause. This, I believe, is the reason behind Paul's Roman imprisonment. It was a result of an action Paul took in the mistaken conviction that he was doing the right thing. One of the most helpful sections we have in the entire Book of Acts is introduced by Luke's account of Paul's mistake. It opens with the story of Paul's last journey to Jerusalem. The apostle and his friends left the Ephesian elders on the beach at Miletus and boarded ship:

> And when we had parted from them and set sail, we came by a straight course to Cos, and the next day to Rhodes, and from there to Patara. And having found a ship crossing to Phoenicia, we went aboard, and set sail. When we had come in sight of Cyprus, leaving it on the left we sailed to Syria, and landed at Tyre; for there the ship was to unload its cargo. And having

sought out the disciples, we stayed there for seven days. Through the Spirit they told Paul not to go on to Jerusalem. And when our days there were ended, we departed and went on our journey; and they all, with wives and children, brought us on our way till we were outside the city; and kneeling down on the beach we prayed and bade one another farewell. Then we went on board the ship, and they returned home (Acts 21:1-6).

As you can see, that is largely an itinerary of the progress of the vessel down the coast of Asia Minor and then across a reach of the Mediterranean toward Jerusalem. It is obviously an eye-witness account. Luke was aboard and was recording the details of their journey. During the voyage they came to the ancient city of Tyre, north of Palestine. There they looked up certain disciples who, through the Spirit, told Paul that he should not go up to Jerusalem.

Hard to Believe

Many commentators have struggled with this passage. I suppose we are all reluctant to attribute any wrongful action to the Apostle Paul. We recognize the strength of his character, the fervor of his spirit, the love and compassion that was always near the surface in this greathearted man, and we have come to love him. It is hard to believe that Paul would ever deliberately disobey the Holy Spirit. And yet, taken at its face value, this sentence indicates a command of the Holy

Spirit which the apostle, for motives we shall examine, chose to ignore.

Many people soften the implications of this sentence and say that it was only another warning of trouble ahead. But the apostle hardly needed any such warning. He well knew that trouble lay ahead of him. Back in chapter 20, verses 22 and 23, in his address to the Ephesian elders, he said,

> And now, behold, I am going to Jerusalem, bound in the Spirit, not knowing what shall befall me there; except that the Holy Spirit testifies to me in every city that imprisonment and afflictions await me.

Paul already understood that he was heading into trouble if he went to Jerusalem, so it seems unlikely that he needed any further warning.

Others say that Paul was right and that it was the disciples who were wrong, that they should not have tried to stop Paul, since he was following an inner leading of the Spirit which they should have acknowledged. But that is to ignore three crucial words: it was *through the Spirit* that they told Paul not to go on to Jerusalem.

We must face the full implications of those words. They were recorded by Luke, who was Paul's friend. He wrote this account several years later, and with the advantages of hindsight he looked back over all the events that followed. And yet, led by the Holy Spirit in recording this inspired book, he wrote down at this juncture that it was through the Holy Spirit that these disciples told Paul he was not to go up to Jerusalem.

The Greek is very strong here—much stronger than our English text. Literally they said, "Stop going up to Jerusalem!" And verse 4, which in our version begins with "And" should really begin with "But," for Luke is recording a contrast here. He says,

> Through the Spirit they told Paul not to go on to Jerusalem. *But* when our days there were ended, we departed and went on our journey. . . .

Well, there is Paul's mistake. He did not follow the clear direction of the Holy Spirit. If we are to understand his action and derive any meaning or benefit from it, we must see where it began. Back in chapter 19 we have a word about the apostle's thoughts when he was still in Ephesus. In verse 21 Luke tells us,

> Now after these events Paul resolved in the Spirit to pass through Macedonia and Achaia and go to Jerusalem, saying, "After I have been there, I must also see Rome."

That was the beginning of Paul's resolve to go to Jerusalem. There was nothing wrong with that at all. Here also Luke records that this was done *in the Spirit;* in other words, it was perfectly proper for Paul to have decided to go up to Jerusalem at this point. God does not always guide us with messages sent before we make a decision. He expects us to make decisions and to step out on the basis of faith to do what looks like the right thing, and to change our minds only if we are impressed by the Spirit or by the Word that a decision is wrong. So there was nothing wrong with Paul's decision at this point.

A little later on, at the beginning of chapter 20, we read that he did go through Macedonia and down into Greece, where he spent three months in the city of Corinth. It was during this three-month period that the apostle wrote the great letter to the Romans. In that letter he tells us what motivated his desire to be in Jerusalem at this time. Before we look at that passage in Romans, we need to note verse 16 in chapter 20. Paul had come back near Ephesus, but, Luke says,

> . . . Paul had decided to sail past Ephesus, so that he might not have to spend time in Asia; for he was hastening to be at Jerusalem, if possible, on the day of Pentecost.

Why did Paul want to be in Jerusalem on the day of Pentecost? The answer is found in the letter to the Romans. In the first part of chapter 9 Paul unfolds to us something of the agony of his heart concerning his people:

> I am speaking the truth in Christ, I am not lying; my conscience bears me witness in the Holy Spirit [three times he affirms the solemnity of what he says], that I have great sorrow and unceasing anguish in my heart. For I could wish that I myself were accursed and cut off from Christ for the sake of my brethren, my kinsmen by race. They are

Israelites, and to them belong the son-
ship, the glory, the covenants, the giv-
ing of the law, the worship, and the
promises; to them belong the patri-
archs, and of their race, according to
the flesh, is the Christ. God who is over
all be blessed forever. Amen (Romans
9:1-5).

It is difficult for Gentiles to understand this
emotion in the Apostle Paul. But he was a Jew,
and as a Jew he loved his nation. He loved their
heritage, their background, and their possession
of the promises of God. He loved all the ritual
and ceremony which had been given to them to
teach them about the coming of the One who
would fulfill the meaning of those observances.
Paul longed to reach the Jews. His heart was
broken as he saw their bitterness and frustration,
and the hostility and opposition to the cause of
Christ which came from his own people. He
knew that at Pentecost there would be a gathering of Jews from all over the Roman empire, and
there was born in his heart a great hunger to be
there.

Israel's Relationship to God

Something further is involved in this; we also
know from Romans that Paul was a prophet. In
chapter 11 he indicated that he well knew that the
welfare of the whole world hung ultimately on
what happened to Israel. That is still true. The
world will never solve its problems until Israel is
in a right relationship to God. And Paul, watching the developing signs of the times in his day,

felt that the day of Christ's return was drawing very near.

We must remember, living as we do two thousand years this side of the apostle's life, that Paul and his associates did not anticipate that the period before the Lord's return would be anywhere near as long as it has been. They couldn't have, for the time was not revealed. As Jesus said, the times and the seasons were not for them to know, just as they are not for us to know. God has always expected his church, in every age, to keep looking for the return of Jesus.

But Paul seems to have made the mistake, as many do today, unfortunately, of reading the signs of the times in the present indicative tense instead of holding them always in the subjunctive—of saying, "It is the time of our Lord's return," instead of, "It may be that this is the time." No one can be certain about the time. Personally, I feel that today could well be the time of our Lord's return. I see many signs which indicate that we are drawing near to it. But no one can say precisely, "This is the time." We need to see that even these apostles—as they neared the end of their lives and saw struggle and strife breaking out in Israel, and knew that the Romans would soon be moving to destroy that nation (as indeed they did in A.D. 70)—might well have thought, "This is the hour when the Lord Jesus is about to return."

Paul did think this, and he was *determined* to be involved in it. He longed to be an instrument to reach his people, and, moved by the anguish of his heart, he began to plan to be in Jerusalem on that day when the Jews would be gathered from all parts of the earth, so that he might have a part in proclaiming to them the kingship and lordship of Jesus Christ over that nation.

Now there was nothing wrong with that part of his motive, absolutely nothing at all. But the account makes it clear that God had chosen otherwise; that God, in his great wisdom, saw that it was not necessary to have Paul in Jerusalem *at this time.* He had given him another ministry. Although Paul had a ministry to Israel and witnessed to them in every city to which he went, his ministry was primarily to the far reaches of the Roman empire, to the Gentiles, and it is clear that the Spirit of God did not want him in Jerusalem. Paul's mistake lay in insisting, out of mistaken zeal, upon doing what his heart longed to do for the glory of Jesus Christ.

A Painful Scene

A second motive is revealed in the next section Luke records for us:

> When we had finished the voyage from Tyre, we arrived at Ptolemais; and we greeted the brethren and stayed with them for one day. On the morrow we departed and came to Caesarea; and we entered the house of Philip the evangelist, who was one of the seven, and stayed with him. And he had four unmarried daughters, who prophesied. While we were staying for some days, a prophet named Agabus came down

from Judea. And coming to us he took Paul's girdle and bound his own feet and hands, and said, "Thus says the Holy Spirit, 'So shall the Jews at Jerusalem bind the man who owns this girdle and deliver him into the hands of the Gentiles.' " When we heard this, we and the people there begged him not to go up to Jerusalem. Then Paul answered, "What are you doing, weeping and breaking my heart? For I am ready not only to be imprisoned but even to die at Jerusalem for the name of the Lord Jesus." And when he would not be persuaded, we ceased and said, "The will of the Lord be done."

After these days we made ready and went up to Jerusalem. And some of the disciples from Caesarea went with us, bringing us to the house of Mnason of Cyprus, an early disciple, with whom we should lodge (Acts 21:7-16).

Had Paul obeyed the Holy Spirit at Tyre, Luke undoubtedly would simply have recorded here what he once wrote about another occasion in Paul's life: "We tried to go up to Jerusalem, but were forbidden of the Holy Spirit," just as once he recorded that the apostle tried to go into Asia and Bithynia, but was forbidden by the Spirit.

But instead we have this rather painful scene. At Caesarea they came into the home of Philip the evangelist, whom we have met before in Acts, the man who led the Ethiopian eunuch to Christ. While he was there, Agabus, a well-known prophet of the Lord whom we have also met before (Acts 11:28), came to speak to Paul. In that dramatic, visual way by which Orientals illustrate truth, he took Paul's sash from around his waist and, binding his own feet and hands, said, "This is what the Holy Spirit is saying to you, Paul. If you go on to Jerusalem, you will be delivered into the hands of the Gentiles. They will bind you, and you'll be a prisoner."

When we connect this with the previous paragraph we can see clearly that this was the last effort the Holy Spirit made to awaken the apostle to what he was doing. Agabus was joined in this by the whole body of believers. The whole family present urged him not to go, including Luke; we read, "When *we* heard this, *we* and the people there begged him not to go up to Jerusalem." So even his close associates recognized the voice of the Spirit, to which the apostle seemed strangely deaf. He refused to listen.

In Paul's reply to them we can detect that, without quite realizing what has happened, he has succumbed to what today we call a "martyr complex." His words are brave and sincere and earnest. He meant every word of them. He said, "Why are you weeping, and breaking my heart? Why do you make it difficult for me? I'm determined to go on to Jerusalem, and I'm ready to die there." We can find no fault with the bravery and courage expressed in those words. But it was not necessary for him to go, and the Spirit had told him *not* to.

Here we see what can happen to a man of God

when he is misled by an urgent hunger to accomplish a goal which God has not given him to do. The flesh had deceived Paul. He apparently saw himself as doing what the Lord did in his final journey up to Jerusalem. The Gospel accounts say that Jesus steadfastly set his face to go there, determined to go against all the pleading and the warnings of his own disciples.

Paul must have seen himself in that role. But Jesus had the Spirit's witness within that this was the will of the Father for him, while Paul had exactly the opposite. The Spirit had made it crystal clear that he was *not* to go to Jerusalem, had finally put it in almost the same terms employed by the angel toward Balaam, who, riding upon his ass, was determined to do *his* own will: "Stop going up to Jerusalem."

When Paul refused to be persuaded, his friends said, "Well, may the will of the Lord be done." That is what you say when you have said all else there is to say. They are simply saying, "Lord, it is up to you. We can't stop this man. He has a strong will and a mighty determination, and he's deluded into thinking that this is what you want. Therefore you will have to handle it. May the will of the Lord be done." The will of the Lord *was* done, and that is what the rest of this account will trace for us.

In the next section we learn of the welcome which Paul and his party received in Jerusalem. Here Luke makes clear what Paul's mistake was *not*. Some scholars feel that perhaps his difficulty was created by a doctrinal error. But I think

Luke has been especially led of the Holy Spirit to record this next section in order to show us that Paul made no such error.

> When we had come to Jerusalem, the brethren received us gladly. On the following day Paul went in with us to James; and all the elders were present. After greeting them, he related one by one the things that God had done among the Gentiles through his ministry. And when they heard it, they glorified God. And they said to him, "You see, brother, how many thousands there are among the Jews of those who have believed; they are all zealous for the law, and they have been told about you that you teach all the Jews who are among the Gentiles to forsake Moses, telling them not to circumcise their children or observe the customs" (Acts 21:17-21).

Many have misread this and concluded that Paul's mistake was that he did not boldly acknowledge that he *did* set aside Moses and the law, that he *did* reject circumcision as of no value whatsoever, as you read in his letters to the Colossians and the Galatians, for example. But the key phrase is, "that you teach all the *Jews*" to do so. That charge was totally false. Paul never taught a Jew to abandon Moses, or not to circumcise his children. What he strongly taught was that the *Gentiles* should not be made subject to these Jewish provisions. He would not allow them to come under the Jewish law, and insisted that they did not have to follow any of these Jewish provisions.

Retelling the Story

But he did not set aside the ritual for the Jews. Rather, he pointed out to them that the ritual was all symbolic, a picture pointing toward Christ. The very rituals they were performing and the sacrifices they were offering were all telling them of Jesus. Jesus' coming had filled out the picture drawn by the Old Testament sacrifices. Thus in the process of carrying them out the Jews were simply reminding themselves of the coming of the Lord Jesus. These observances were very much like the Lord's table is for us today. In that ritual we know that we are dealing with symbols which are retelling the story of the life and death and resurrection of Jesus. Doing this does not give us any added spirituality. In itself it does not make us any better, but it reminds us.

The function of these Jewish rituals, then, was to remind them of what the Lord Jesus had come to do, and had done. All through the Book of Acts we see Jewish Christians going into the temple and performing ceremonies, just as the Lord Himself had done. There is no suggestion that they should have stopped, or that it was wrong for them to do this, until God took the rituals away.

The Jewish sacrifices ended when the temple was finally destroyed in A.D. 70, when the words of Jesus were fulfilled and Roman armies came and laid seige to the city. His words of warning

were, "When you see Jerusalem surrounded by
armies, then flee into the mountains, for then
shall be fulfilled all that has been predicted."
The city was taken and the Jews were carried
away captive, exactly as the Lord Jesus said. But
that was still several years in the future from this
point in history. So Paul is not compromising
when, as we read in this next section, he took
upon himself certain Jewish practices. James
said to him,

> "What then is to be done? They will
> certainly hear that you have come. Do
> therefore what we tell you. We have
> four men who are under a vow; take
> these men and purify yourself along
> with them and pay their expenses, so
> that they may shave their heads. Thus
> all will know that there is nothing in
> what they have been told about you but
> that you yourself live in observance of
> the law. But as for the Gentiles who
> have believed, we have sent a letter with
> our judgment that they should abstain
> from what has been sacrificed to idols
> and from blood and from what is
> strangled and from unchastity." Then
> Paul took the men, and the next day he
> purified himself with them and went in-
> to the temple, to give notice when the
> days of purification would be fulfilled
> and the offering presented for every
> one of them (Acts 21:22-26).

Here Paul was following his own announced
practice. He wrote that when he was with the

Jews, he became as a Jew; when he was with the Gentiles, he became as a Gentile; and when he was with the weak, he limited himself and became as weak as they—all in order that he might reach them on their level, through the medium and culture to which they were accustomed. He was simply declaring again the freedom he had in Christ. He was free—free to live as a Gentile among the Gentiles, free to live as a Jew among the Jews—free from the law, but free also to keep the law if there were certain advantages to be gained for the sake of the gospel by so doing.

So Paul adopts this Jewish practice, willing to become as a Jew, along with these others, in order to clear up a misunderstanding which had a totally false basis. As you read the account which follows of the trouble he met in Jerusalem, you can see that not one bit of it was a consequence of his Jewish practices. The trouble that broke out, as we will see in our next chapter, was due simply to his presence in Jerusalem, where he had no business being.

No Guarantee Against Failure

There is a deep lesson here for us, one which strikes particularly deep into my own heart. It is this: experience, even long-continued Christian experience, along with spiritual insight and understanding of Scripture, are no guarantees against failure—against missing the mind of God. That is why we often see men and women who have been greatly used of God for years and years, suddenly fail in some way and cast a blot upon their ministry. This again indicates to us the deadliness of our enemy. The flesh can bide its time. It can wait out long periods of subjugation, or relative victory in Christ, and then catch us off guard—especially by awakening a desire which seems to be right, seems to be exactly what God would want done.

Now the Spirit of God is always faithful to warn us. We need not stumble blindly into this trap, any more than Paul needed to. But what this great study shows us is that we must be very careful to be obedient to the Spirit's voice. When he blocks our plans, clearly and unmistakably, we are to obey. Otherwise we simply open ourselves up to unnecessary heartache, unnecessary limitation and restriction, as the apostle did here.

But God did not abandon or forsake Paul. He picked him up and used him powerfully, turning the mistake itself into opportunities for the advance of his cause. But Paul himself had to undergo deprivation, heartache, and suffering which he need not have endured if he had been obedient to the Holy Spirit. Through this experience God helps us to learn that even a mighty apostle can fail in faith at times. May this serve as a lesson to us that only as we walk in obedience to the voice of God and to the clear directions of the Word of God can we find our way through all the pitfalls that await us in life.

CHAPTER TWO

TROUBLE AT JERUSALEM

Acts 21:27—22:29

To allay the suspicions of the Jews about
Paul's teaching, he had assumed the responsibility of going into the temple with four young men
who had taken a Nazarite vow, and of paying
their expenses until they could complete the
prescribed rites and shave their heads. It was
when this was nearly accomplished that trouble
began. Luke continues the account, beginning
with verse 27:

> When the seven days were almost com-
> pleted, the Jews from Asia, who had
> seen him in the temple, stirred up all the
> crowd, and laid hands on him, crying
> out, "Men of Israel, help! This is the
> man who is teaching men everywhere
> against the people and the law and this
> place; moreover he also brought Greeks
> into the temple, and he has defiled this
> holy place." For they had previously
> seen Trophimus the Ephesian with him
> in the city, and they supposed that Paul
> had brought him into the temple (Acts
> 21:27-29).

Notice who instigates this trouble. It is not the
Jews in Jerusalem; it is those from Asia. The
capital of the Roman province of Asia was

Ephesus. So it was undoubtedly the same Jews who had caused the disturbance in Ephesus which resulted in a riot that drove Paul out of the city. Here they are again, hot on his trail, these riot engineers traveling around from place to place, deliberately stirring up trouble, determined to destroy the tremendous work of the apostle.

Naturally they were upset by what had happened in Ephesus. The liberating power of the gospel had hit that region with such impact that it had demolished the structure of the superstitious pagan worship in that city. As a result, the trade of the idol-making silversmiths fell off, and so they rioted, led by a man named Demetrius. And now here they are in Jerusalem. Very likely Alexander the coppersmith, who had caused Paul so much trouble in Ephesus, is here as well.

It is quite evident that the Lord Jesus had wanted Paul to avoid this trouble. This is why he had said through the Spirit that Paul was not to go to Jerusalem; he knew these troublemakers were there. He knew the volatile character of the Jewish nation. He read, far more clearly than Paul, the stubborn resistance of the Jewish heart to the gospel, and he knew that any attempt to reach this stubborn people would be hopeless at this time. But Paul could not see that.

The Lord would have allowed Paul to continue his great ministry throughout the Gentile regions, where he now had a freedom he never experienced in the early part of his ministry.

After the decision made by the Roman judge at Corinth, Paul had access to every Roman city to preach the gospel, and he could have gone on proclaiming Christ in liberty. But now his presence in Jerusalem makes him subject to attack and awakens the possibility of this riot.

Explosive Charges

Notice the palpably false charge thrown against Paul. It is purely circumstantial, cooked up out of false evidence. He is charged with being against the religion of Judaism. Further, the Jews invent the accusation that Paul has defiled the temple by bringing Gentiles into it. Some years ago an archeologist exploring the ruins of Jerusalem dug up the actual copper plaque which had been affixed to the wall that divided the court of the Gentiles from the inner temple courts available only to Jews. It stated, both in Greek and Hebrew, that any Gentile daring to set foot beyond this wall was subject immediately to the penalty of death. So the Jews were incensed at the very idea of any violation of the temple. And, since they had seen Paul with a Greek in the streets of Jerusalem, they reasoned, "Well, if Paul would walk down the street with a Gentile, he would also take him into the temple." That was enough to cause an immediate explosion.

> Then all the city was aroused, and the people ran together; they seized Paul and dragged him out of the temple, and at once the gates were shut. And as they were trying to kill him, word came to

the tribune of the cohort that all Jerusalem was in confusion. He at once took soldiers and centurions, and ran down to them; and when they saw the tribune and the soldiers, they stopped beating Paul. Then the tribune came up and arrested him, and ordered him to be bound with two chains. He inquired who he was and what he had done. Some in the crowd shouted one thing, some another; and as he could not learn the facts because of the uproar, he ordered him to be brought into the barracks. And when he came to the steps, he was actually carried by the soldiers because of the violence of the crowd; for the mob of the people followed, crying "Away with him!" (Acts 21:30-36).

It is obvious that Luke is an eyewitness to this stirring and colorful scene. No description in the New Testament is more dramatic that this one. A few years ago I stood in Jerusalem on the site of the Roman fortress of Antonia, overlooking the temple courts. Looking down into that arena I tried to reproduce in my imagination this vivid, colorful, tumultuous scene, as the whole area, packed with Jews gathered for the great day of the feast, had churned in turmoil, enraged by the accusation that Paul had brought Greeks into the sacred temple courts. They seized him and began to beat him with their fists and kick him with their feet, trying to knock him down so they could stamp the life out of him.

They were prevented only by the intervention of the Roman guards. The sentries on the wall, seeing the tumult, sent word to their commander, the Roman tribune whose name, Claudius Lysias, is given a little later in Acts. Evidently the governor was in the capital of Caesarea, down on the coast, and Claudius Lysias was in charge of Jerusalem. When the word came he immediately took centurions (captains of hundreds) and gathered perhaps two or three hundred soldiers and charged down into this crowd.

They shouldered their way through the enraged mob, surrounded the apostle, and picked him up and carried him out on their shoulders. The crowd was so enraged that they battled the soldiers all the way. Even this large force could rescue the apostle only with the greatest difficulty. The Romans to the rescue! What a tremendous scene this was! Paul was near death at this point. The mob had actually begun to beat him to death.

Bold Request

But next we have an amazing account which shows the courage of this great apostle. He makes a bold request of the centurion:

> As Paul was about to be brought into the barracks, he said to the tribune, "May I say something to you?" And he said, "Do you know Greek? Are you not the Egyptian, then, who recently stirred up a revolt and led the four thousand men of the Assassins out into

the wilderness?'' Paul replied, ''I am a Jew, from Tarsus in Cilicia, a citizen of no mean city; I beg you, let me speak to the people.'' And when he had given him leave, Paul, standing on the steps, motioned with his hand to the people; and when there was a great hush, he spoke to them in the Hebrew language . . . (Acts 21:37-40).

How remarkable that Paul would ask permission to speak to this enraged mob, which had just been ready to tear him limb from limb! I am sure that if I had been in his shoes I would have been trying to get out of there as quickly as possible, quite content to let the mob go. But Paul recognizes this as his opportunity. He has come to Jerusalem *determined* to speak to his nation. Out of the urgency of his love for them he wants to be the instrument to reach this stubborn crowd. So he seizes the only opportunity he has, hoping the Lord will give him success.

The tribune is very startled when Paul addresses him in Greek, because this rough Roman officer thought he knew who Paul was. He thought he was that Egyptian who, according to Josephus, a year or so earlier had led a band of desperate men out to the Mount of Olives, promising them that he had the power to cause the walls of Jerusalem to fall down at his command. Of course he was unable to deliver on his promise, and the Romans had made short work of the rebels, killing most of them, except for the Egyptian leader, who had escaped.

But when this tribune heard the cultured accents of Greece he knew that Paul was no Assassin. (The rebels were called that because they had concealed daggers in their cloaks, and as they mingled among the people they would strike without warning, killing people at random in cold blood. They were utter terrorists, trying to strike dread into the Jewish populace and thus to overthrow the Roman government.) And so, impressed by something about the apostle, the tribune lets him speak to this crowd. Amazingly, when Paul indicates with his hand that he wants to speak, a great hush falls.

To Win a Hearing

Now we have Paul's defense, in chapter 22. We get the introduction in the first five verses:

> "Brethren and fathers, hear the defense which I now make before you."

> And when they heard that he addressed them in the Hebrew language, they were the more quiet. And he said: "I am a Jew, born at Tarsus in Cilicia, but brought up in this city at the feet of Gamaliel, educated according to the strict manner of the law of our fathers, being zealous for God as you all are this day. I persecuted this Way to the death, binding and delivering to prison both men and women, as the high priest and the whole council of elders bear me witness. From them I received letters to the brethren, and I journeyed to Damascus to take those also who were there and

bring them in bonds to Jerusalem to be
punished'' (Acts 22:1-5).

Everything in this paragraph is cleverly yet
earnestly designed to win a hearing for what the
apostle has to say. He reminds them that he himself is a Jew. He speaks to them in their own language, Aramaic, a dialect of Hebrew, which was
spoken throughout the city. He says he was born
in the fine university city of Tarsus, and brings in
the honored name of Gamaliel, his great teacher.
Gamaliel, who had died only a year or two
before, was one of five Jewish rabbis regarded as
the greatest of all time. His nickname was "The
Beauty of the Law," so highly was he honored
by these Jews because of his insight and understanding of the Old Testament Scriptures. Paul is
trying to impress the people that he was tutored
at the feet of this godly man, in order to make
them listen.

He goes on from there to tell them the simple
story of his conversion:

"As I made my journey and drew near
to Damascus, about noon a great light
from heaven suddenly shone about me.
And I fell to the ground and heard a
voice saying to me, 'Saul, Saul, why do
you persecute me?' And I answered,
'Who are you, Lord?' And he said to
me, 'I am Jesus of Nazareth whom you
are persecuting.' Now those who were
with me saw the light but did not hear
the voice of the one who was speaking
to me. And I said, 'What shall I do,

Lord?' And the Lord said to me, 'Rise, and go into Damascus, and there you will be told all that is appointed for you to do.' And when I could not see because of the brightness of that light, I was led by the hand by those who were with me, and came into Damascus'' (Acts 22:6-11).

The apostle makes no attempt to preach to these people, but instead falls back upon what is basically the most powerful form of witness—simple testimony as to what had happened to him. That is very solid ground. Whenever you give your witness, your testimony of what Jesus Christ has done for you and of how he has changed your life, you are the world's greatest authority on that subject. So Paul could speak with absolutely unassailable logic and conviction. He simply recounts the story, doing his best to lay hold of the hearts of these stubborn Jews. He tells them that despite his hostility to Christianity he was converted against his will. This is the testimony of a hostile witness, which in a court of law carries greater weight than any other kind. What an arresting effect the story must have had upon this crowd, which had never before heard it from his own lips! Then he recites his commission as an apostle:

"And one Ananias, a devout man according to the law, well spoken of by all the Jews who lived there, came to me and standing by me said to me, 'Brother Saul, receive your sight' '' (Acts 26:12,13).

I have always been impressed with the courage of Ananias. How would you like to be sent to Public Enemy Number One, to the head of the Mafia, to welcome him, put your arms around him, and call him "brother?" Paul goes on:

> "And in that very hour I received my sight and saw him. And he said, 'The God of our fathers appointed you to know his will, to see the Just One and to hear a voice from his mouth; for you will be a witness for him to all men of what you have seen and heard. And now why do you wait? Rise and be baptized, and wash away your sins, calling on his name' " (Acts 26:13-16).

Notice how the details of this event are etched into the apostle's memory. Though it occurred thirty years before, he has never forgotten a single detail. He recalls it all as vividly as if it had happened yesterday. This was the moment he was chosen to be an apostle, and Ananias conveyed the commission to him. It had three parts, three aspects of ministry, as Paul clearly details.

Pattern Christian

First, he was chosen to know the will the God, and from that he obtained the power by which he was to minister. Paul was sent out as a pattern Christian. That is what apostles are. They are not special people living at a high level of spiritual life, to which none of us can ever expect to attain. They live at the very level we are to live on. The first thing that Paul was taught was to know the will of God. That did not mean that Paul was to know where God wanted him to go, or what God wanted him to do. What Paul had to learn was that the will of God is a relationship to his Son. When Paul understood that, he had all the power he needed to do anything God asked him to do. *That* is the will of God.

I find that many Christians struggle at this point. They think that the will of God is some kind of itinerary they must discover, that if they can just find where God wants them to go, and what He wants them to do next, then they can do the will of God. No, the Scriptures make clear that the will of God is a relationship. It is your attitude of expectancy that Jesus Christ, living in you, will work through you. When you expect him to do that, you are in the will of God. Do anything you like, then, because it will be God's will, unless the Holy Spirit within you indicates otherwise, according to His Word. That is what Paul learned—the power by which a Christian lives his life.

Then on that basis, he was to see the Just One, the Lord Jesus. Paul looks back and says, "This is what made me an apostle. I have seen Jesus Christ many times. He has appeared to me, and talked to me. He told me, directly and personally, the things that the other apostles learned when they were with Him as disciples. That is how I know them." And, motivated by the love of Jesus Christ and an awareness of the majesty of his Person, Paul pushed on ceaselessly, out into the far regions of earth, performing his apostolic ministry.

Finally, Paul was to hear a voice from the Lord's mouth. That was his message—to declare what Jesus Christ had said to him. It was the same message Jesus had given to the twelve, in the days of his flesh. That is how they knew that Paul was a true apostle—because he knew what they knew. God has the same message for all of us today—the words of his mouth, which Jesus had given to the Apostle Paul.

Confrontation at Jerusalem

In the next section Paul strangely includes the confrontation he had with Jesus in Jerusalem:

> "When I had returned to Jerusalem and was praying in the temple, I fell into a trance and saw Him saying to me, 'Make haste and get quickly out of Jerusalem, because they will not accept your testimony about me.' And I said, 'Lord, they themselves know that in every synagogue I imprisoned and beat those who believe in thee. And when the blood of Stephen thy witness was shed, I also was standing by and approving, and keeping the garments of those who killed him.' And he said to me, 'Depart; for I will send you far away to the Gentiles' " (Acts 22:17-21).

It is strange that Paul should recount this episode on this occasion. Perhaps he is trying to explain why he ultimately went to the Gentiles. But in a sense he is testifying against himself here. This episode had occurred some 27 years earlier, when, three years after his conversion, he came back to Jerusalem to be the self-styled apostle to Israel and to preach to this nation about Jesus Christ. In Damascus, convinced that he was equipped with all it took to reach Israel with the gospel, he ended up having to escape the city by being let down over the walls in a basket. Though discouraged by that, he still thought he would get somewhere in Jerusalem. He came there to preach to Israel, but even the Christians would not receive him. The apostles would have nothing to do with him.

Brokenhearted, he came into the temple to pray. There the Lord Jesus met him and said, "Get out of Jerusalem. Make haste, get out! They will not accept your testimony!" The strange thing is that, 27 years later, here he is in Jerusalem again, and Jesus is saying the very same thing to him: "Get out! They will not accept your testimony. You should not have gone up to Jerusalem." Though Paul had been warned through the Spirit he had tried anyway, and now he has come to exactly the same place. One word about going to the Gentiles, and the place explodes—blows up in his face:

> Up to this word they listened to him;
> then they lifted up their voices and said,
> "Away with such a fellow from the
> earth! For he ought not to live." And
> as they cried out and waved their gar-
> ments and threw dust in the air, the
> tribune commanded him to be brought
> into the barracks, and ordered him to
> be examined by scourging, to find out

> why they shouted thus against him
> (Acts 22:22-24).

This poor tribune has not understood a word
that Paul has said to these people, because he has
spoken in Aramaic. And when the place all of a
sudden erupts he does not know what to make of
it. So he thinks, "We'll get the truth out of him
—we'll scourge it out of him!" This was a brutal
and bloody process of beating a man on the bare
back with leather thongs in which were imbedded
pieces of metal and bone. It would have torn
Paul's back to a bloody pulp. That was the cruel
method the Romans used.

Distortion of the Divine Plan

But we are told here what had offended these
Jews. The point of pride which Paul had touched
was the idea that God would even consider going
to the Gentiles and bringing them into the same
blessings the Jews had enjoyed. Their racist re-
jection of this notion was complete. But what a
twisting and distorting of the divine program
that represented! The nation Israel had been
called of God to be the vehicle by which the nations should be reached! But instead of obeying
that call they had selfishly gathered it all to themselves and said, "God has chosen us; therefore
we must be a superior people. He doesn't have
any interest in the rest of the world. Let all the
Gentiles go to hell; *we're* the people of God, the
chosen instruments of God! And we don't like
anybody who suggests that God is going to save
those dirty dogs, the Gentiles, on the same basis

that he does us Jews!''

This was the rankest form of racial prejudice, on a par with the worst of the hatred of whites for blacks in our country today. But what strikes me as I read this account is how closely it resembles much of the evangelical isolationism which the church has been going through. To a great degree we have done the same thing. We have felt that God is not interested in the world, that he wants only us, that we are the favored people of God. We have gathered our robes of self-righteousness about ourselves and drawn into our Christian ghettos and said, ''Let the world go to hell! We are going to enjoy God's favor and blessing.'' And we have resisted the chance to reach out to the lost, fragmented humanity around us.

But God always judges that. He is judging it in our day. He judges this self-righteous pride which says, ''We are espeically favored,'' which refuses to recognize that we are nothing but guilty sinners like anybody else, and are just enjoying the *grace* of God. That grace is as much available to anybody, anywhere, as it is to us. We have the responsibility to share it!

The last section shows the protection God provided for his apostle:

> But when they had tied him up with the thongs, Paul said to the centurion who was standing by, ''Is it lawful for you to scourge a man who is a Roman citizen, and uncondemned?'' When the centurion heard that, he went to the tri-

bune and said to him, "What are you about to do? For this man is a Roman citizen." So the tribune came and said to him, "Tell me, are you a Roman citizen?" And he aid, "Yes." The tribune answered, "I bought this citizenship for a large sum." Paul said, "But I was born a citizen." [A bit of one-upmanship here.] So those who were about to examine him withdrew from him instantly; and the tribune also was afraid, for he realized that Paul was a Roman citizen and that he had bound him (Acts 22:25-29).

The law of Rome said explicitly that no Roman was to be bound without due process of law. Furthermore, they were not to be beaten under any circumstances, even if convicted. The penalty for doing so was death. So this tribune knew he was in trouble. He was very frightened when he learned that Paul was a citizen and realized that he had both bound Paul and was on the very verge of beating him with the terrible, bloody scourge. Here God used the state to protect his apostle. The state is also the instrument of God, and we must remember that. The powers that be are ordained of God, and God uses them —as he did in this case to preserve the life of Paul.

As we review this account I cannot help but think of the phrase Paul uses in his second letter to the Corinthians: "struck down but not destroyed." God will sometimes let us stumble in our folly into disasters from which we must suffer, sometimes for days and weeks and months and years. But he never abandons us. He never leaves us all alone. He finds a way to work it all out and he brings us back.

In our next study we will see how graciously the Lord Jesus restores his mighty apostle. Though he must remain a prisoner of Caesar, in the hands of the Roman authorities, nevertheless he will be permitted to carry on his great ministry in power and blessing, with renewed influence througout the Roman empire. God never abandons his people!

CHAPTER THREE

LOVE THAT NEVER LETS GO

Acts 22:30—23:35

At the end of chapter 22, Paul is in the hands of a very puzzled Roman tribune who cannot figure out what to do with this civilized, cultured man with the ability to speak in several languages, a Roman citizen from the honored university city of Tarsus. Everytime Paul comes in contact with the Jews there is an explosion. Like putting steel to a grinder, putting Paul in the presence of these Jews makes sparks fly. The tribune does not understand this strange reaction, but he is going to try again.

> But on the morrow, desiring to know the real reason why the Jews accused him, he [the Roman tribune] unbound him, and commanded the chief priests and all the council to meet, and he brought Paul down and set him before them (Acts 22:30).

The tribune summons the high priests and the elders—the Sanhedrin—to the Roman fortress of Antonia. Then he brings Paul down and sets him in their midst. And now Paul has an occasion to address the leaders of the nation, the representatives of the people. We get his introduction at the beginning of chapter 23:

> And Paul, looking intently at the council, said, "Brethren, I have lived before God in all good conscience up to this day." And the high priest Ananias commanded those who stood by him to strike him on the mouth. Then Paul said to him, "God shall strike you, you whitewashed wall! Are you sitting to judge me according to the law, and yet contrary to the law you order me to be struck?" Those who stood by said, "Would you revile God's high priest?" And Paul said, "I did not know, brethren, that he was the high priest; for it is written, 'You shall not speak evil of a ruler of your people' " (Acts 23:1-5).

What a left-footed beginning! There is a noticeably reckless audacity about the apostle's introduction. He seems to be careless, almost, of the consequences of what he says—like a man burning his bridges behind him. I rather suspect that he is aware by now that he has blundered into a very untenable situation, so he is trying to bull his way through.

You will notice that he does not begin with his usual courtesy. The customary address to the Sanhedrin was a standardized form which began, "Rulers of Israel, and elders of the people. . . ." Paul does not employ that, as he normally would, but instead puts himself right on a level with these rulers, doubtless because he was once one of them, and he addresses them simply with the familiar term, "Brethren."

Now that was an offense to these Jews. It was

true that Paul once belonged to them. Perhaps he knew many of them personally. But it had been many years since he had ever sat with them. And he well knew, as they did, that a long-standing enmity had arisen between them. And now to have him come and rather brashly address them as his equals was offensive. In addition, he implies that there is no possible ground of complaint against him. He says, "I have lived in all good conscience before God up to this day." This was certainly true. Yet it seemed to imply that there was no reason for this meeting at all—that it was absurd and ridiculous to have called this council together.

Insult and Retort

So for this seeming impudence and impertinence, the high priest commands that Paul be slapped across the mouth. That was an unusually degrading form of insult to an Israelite. The law commanded that no Israelite should ever be struck in the face, and so this was certainly wrong. We Gentiles don't appreciate it very much either.

Paul's anger flashes out at this offense. He whips back the caustic retort, "God shall strike you, you whitewashed wall!" That was a typically Judaistic way of calling the high priest a bare-faced hypocrite. The only whitewashed walls in Israel were tombs. Jesus used this figure when he said to the Pharisees, "You are like tombs, whitewashed on the outside, but within full of dead men's bones." So the apostle is calling him a stinking hypocrite, and this is not lost upon the high priest. It certainly is not the most tactful way for a prisoner to address a judge!

It is very likely that Paul recognized who Ananias was, but not what his position was. Paul knew that Ananias had a reputation as a glutton, a thief, and a stool-pigeon to the Romans. So Paul is offended by the fact that this notorious hypocrite would command him to be struck like this, contrary to the law. But what he did not know was that Ananias had recently been appointed high priest. The council had been convened rather summarily and the priest had probably not had time to dress in his robes.

The moment it is pointed out to him that Ananias is indeed the high priest, Paul is instantly repentant, for he recognizes that he is in the wrong. He apologizes, for the law says that the office deserves respect, even if the man does not. But it is too late; he has already blown his chance. We are accustomed to seeing Peter with his foot in his mouth, but it is rather unusual to find Paul in this condition. But here he is. He has insulted the ruler of the tribunal, making it impossible to receive anything approaching a fair trial.

And yet, it is only what we might have expected. We must bear in mind through this whole study that the apostle has gone to Jerusalem in direct disobedience of a command of the Holy Spirit. He has thereby put himself in the position of being mastered and controlled by the flesh, that principle of evil inherent in every one of us. Remember that the Apostle Paul himself is the one who tells us, in his letter to the Romans, that if we yield ourselves as servants to the flesh, we become the servant of that which we obey.

In other words, if we give way to our insistence on our own stubborn will as opposed to something God has made clear, no matter in what area, we have fallen victim to the flesh, and the flesh rules. Then, even when we *want* to walk in the Spirit in other areas and relationships of our life, we cannot. As a result, the manifestations of the flesh come out, unbidden and against our will. The flesh always carries us farther than we want to go. It sits at the controls of our life and rules us, whether we like it or not. As Paul says in another place, we thus give Satan an advantage over us; no matter what we try to do, it all comes out fleshly.

Prideful Disdain

That is what is happening here. Though Paul is trying to walk in the Spirit he cannot, because the flesh is in command. There are certain unmistakable marks of fleshliness which you see right here in this account. One is a certain prideful disdain of others. Paul is usually the most sensitive of men to the requirement for normal courtesies. But here he sets that aside as he roughly addresses the Sanhedrin.

Ordinarily, recognizing that their position was given by God, he would have used the courteous address their office demanded, as Jesus always did when he spoke to them. But now, with that little touch of disdain, revealing that he obviously thinks of himself as the equal of these men, he adresses them as brethren—much to the offense of these officials, who regard him as a prisoner awaiting judgment.

And there is his obvious testiness, his irritability and quick temper, the flash of anger with which he retorts. His reply is not that of a man in control of his emotions. I well know from my own experience that this is a mark of the flesh in control. There are times when I am resistant to the will of God but try to walk in the Spirit anyway, without settling the matter. At such times I find myself quick of temper, impatient, and caustic. I do not want to be, but I am. That is how Paul is here.

Then you notice that he relies now upon his own wits to get out of this dilemma instead of resting upon the wisdom of God:

> But when Paul perceived that one part were Sadducees and the other Pharisees, he cried out in the council, "Brethren, I am a Pharisee, a son of Pharisees; with respect to the hope and the resurrection of the dead I am on trial." And when he had said this, a dissension arose between the Pharisees and the Sadducees; and the assembly was divided. For the Sadducees say that there is no resurrection, nor angel, nor spirit; but the Pharisees acknowledge them all. Then a great clamor arose; and some of the scribes of the Pharisees' party stood up and contended, "We find nothing wrong in this

man. What if a spirit or an angel spoke
to him?'' And when the dissension became violent, the tribune, afraid that
Paul would be torn in pieces by them,
commanded the soldiers to go down
and take him by force from among
them and bring him into the barracks
(Acts 23:6-10).

I do not think this attempt to divert the subject
was a deliberate trick by the apostle. It was not
some cunning stratagem that he employed to get
himself off the hook by dividing the assembly.
He simply realized that he was in deeper than he
had intended and saw that his cause was lost. So,
hoping for some support from the Pharisees, he
cried out this way, identifying himself with them.

The Pharisees represented at least some adher-
ence to the letter and teaching of the law. The
Sadduccees, on the other hand, were what we
would call modernists, liberals. They denied the
supernatural. They refused to recognize the exis-
tence of angels or spirits, and certainly not the
resurrection from the dead, whereas the Pharisees were more fundamental in their understanding, recognizing that these things were realities.
So they were ready to defend Paul on the ground
that, in his conversion, a spirit might have
spoken to him, or an angel. They were not ready
to acknowledge that it was indeed the Lord
Jesus, but they were at least willing to acknowledge that perhaps something supernatural had
occurred.

Another Screaming Squabble

Paul is simply trying his best, using his wits to get out of his circumstance. But when the flesh is in control, things always work out wrong. We try to take advantage of the situation as we see it. But we always get deeper and deeper into trouble. Paul succeeds only in polarizing the council. His hopes for a testimony before the leaders of the nation fly out the window, and he finds himself in the middle of another screaming squabble of Jews. They are yelling theological arguments at one another and threatening to tear Paul apart as they literally pull and tug at him like a bone of contention.

Once again this puzzled Roman tribune must rescue Paul. Three times now he has pulled him out of the fire. He is getting to be an expert at it, but it completely baffles him. What is it about this man that precipitates an explosion every time he comes into contact with the Jews?

And poor Paul! I think that out of friendship for him Luke hides some of the painful details from us. But you can imagine how Paul must have felt. He had his chance, and he blew it! Now he sits in his cell—utterly humiliated, dejected, defeated, deflated, disenchanted. All his dreams of testimony to the Jews lie in ashes around his feet. Paul is utterly discouraged.

Now that is always God's hour. God waits for a man to arrive at that place. This is the way He heals us after we have moved forward in the self-sufficiency of the flesh. He always lets it run its course until we find ourselves broken, deflated, and dejected—utterly bankrupt. That is God's hour.

Remember how Jesus began the Sermon on the Mount: "Happy are the poor in spirit, for theirs is the kingdom of heaven." Happy are you when you arrive at personal, spiritual bankruptcy, when you do not have any resources left, when you have come to the end of yourself.

I have been there; haven't you? I have said to God, "Lord, I quit! I'm not going to be a Christian anymore. I can't make it. I've tried. I've done everything I know how, and I just can't make it. I'm going to quit." I didn't realize it at the time, but the Lord was standing there saying, "Great! That's just where I wanted you to come, just what I've been waiting for. Now it's my turn."

Restored to Usefulness

That is what happens here. We have seen Paul before the council. Now we see him before the Lord:

> The following night the Lord stood by him and said, "Take courage, for as you have testified about me at Jerusalem, so you must bear witness also at Rome" (Acts 23:11).

Literally, what the Lord Jesus says as he appears to him is, "Be of good cheer. Cheer up, Paul." That is certainly a revelation of the state of Paul's heart at this time. He is anything but of good cheer. He is defeated and discouraged, wallowing in an awful sense of shame and failure, but he is not abandoned. Isn't it wonderful that the Lord comes now to retore him to his ministry?

I am sure that, as in other places, Luke does not give us the full account of what transpired between Paul and his Lord on that night. But there is enough here so that we can see what our Lord is after. He restores Paul to usefulness. He says to him, "As you have testified about me at Jerusalem, so you must bear witness also at Rome." Thus he promises Paul success in the desire of his heart which was second only to his desire to win his kinsmen. He was to have his chance to bear witness for Christ at the heart of the empire, the very capital of the Gentile world.

And yet the very form of expression used by the Lord contains a hint of the limitation resulting from Paul's disobedience. The Lord Jesus puts it this way: *"As* you have testified about me in Jerusalem, *so* you must bear witness also in Rome." In other words, the emphasis here is upon the manner in which this witness will go forth. "In the way you bore witness to me in Jerusalem, *in that same way* you must bear witness in Rome."

How had he testified in Jerusalem? As a prisoner—chained, bound, limited. If Paul had obeyed, he would yet have been free to travel around the Roman world, preaching the gospel. But he disobeyed, so he was permitted to bear witness, but only as a prisoner.

This encounter with the Lord Jesus must have been a wonderful moment in the apostle's experience. The Lord restored him to spiritual health, as he often must do with us. Have you ever disobeyed God, knowing that you shouldn't have but wanting something so badly that you've gone ahead anyway? How wonderful to have the Lord ready to restore us. I have been there too, so I know how God can patiently, tenderly deal with us and bring us back to the place of yieldedness.

After this Paul is his usual self again, and yet he is bound. Ahead of him, before he even comes to Rome, lies two years of confinement in Caesarea. (Nothing is recorded of his ministry during this time, although I am sure he had one.) And after he arrives at Rome he is a prisoner there at least another three years. And yet in this moment the power of Paul's ministry is given back to him. From here on the things he says and does have that same wonderful infusion of the Spirit's power which makes unusual things happen. And from Rome Paul is to write some of his greatest letters—letters filled with power, letters which are still changing the history of the world. The joy of the Lord is back in Paul's heart; the glory returns to his ministry. The love of Jesus Christ is filling him and flooding Paul, empowering and enriching him.

The Scar Remains

The limitation of chains is the resulting scar of sin, the consequence of Paul's disobedience. Young Christians often feel that there is no great problem involved when they deliberately do something wrong. They feel that they can simply confess and come back, and the Lord will forgive them and everything will be fine again. And this much is true: they can be forgiven; they can come back immediately. God does not hold their sin against them; he does not deprive them of their power or of the love, the joy, the fellowship, and the glory of their Christian life. He never wants us to look back upon our past with guilt, in self-abnegation and shame. He wants us to accept the forgiving hand he offers us in the moment of restoration.

That is the glory of being a Christian. You do not have to wait to be forgiven, and you do not have to pay for anything. You do not have to go back and try to placate God in some way because of what you have done. You must make it right, as far as you can, with any people you have wronged, but you can be forgiven and all the glory of your relationship with the Lord restored.

But there is one thing you cannot do: you cannot take away—and God does not take away—the natural results which follow evil. Certain limitations and weaknesses are there, and you must work within them from then on.

You can see this also in the story of Moses. Moses lost his temper in front of the children of Isreal and spoke out hastily. As a result God's cause was greatly damaged. And God said to him, "Because you have done this, you cannot enter the land." Moses was forgiven. His heart was made strong in the Lord again, and the power of his ministry was given back to him. But he was never permitted to enter the land. And even though Moses longed to do so, and asked God to take that restriction away, yet God never rescinded that limitation.

The same kind of thing happened to David. David committed the twin sins of murder and adultery. He was awfully torn by this himself, and he damaged the whole nation by this behavior. God came to David, forgiving and restoring him. He allowed him to keep his throne, and he gave back his power, his joy, his peace, and his love. But God said to him, "David, because you have done this, you will never again have peace in your household." And he never did. His family was fragmented from that moment on, and there was unending trouble in the palace from then on—because of David's evil.

Yes, sin does leave scars. Paul's situation is another example of this truth. His disobedience means that he must be a prisoner. And though he can exercise power and love and joy and peace again with all the fullness he ever had, it will be within the limitation of being bound to a Roman soldier day and night for the next five years or more.

Luke resumes the account and shows us how God's hand now starts to work out his purpose for his restored apostle. A plot begins to develop:

> When it was day, the Jews made a plot and bound themselves by an oath neither to eat nor drink till they had killed Paul. There were more than forty

who made this conspiracy. And they
went to the chief priests and elders, and
said, "We have strictly bound ourselves
by an oath to taste no food till we have
killed Paul. You therefore, along with
the council, give notice now to the
tribune to bring him down to you, as
though you were going to determine his
case more exactly. And we are ready to
kill him before he comes near" (Acts
23:12-15).

This certainly underscores the hopelessness of
Paul's attempt to witness to these Jews. They are
not only unwilling to listen, they are intent upon
killing him. So they concoct a plot by which they
can get Paul away from the protection of the
Roman guardhouse and down into the streets of
Jerusalem on his way to the high priest's palace.
There, in the narrow, tortuous alleyways of that
old city, they have a band of forty men who have
vowed never to eat or drink until they have over-
powered Paul's guards and put him to death. It looks
as if the plot might work. But in the next section
you see God's protection of his apostle, first in
private:

Now the son of Paul's sister heard of
their ambush; so he went and entered
the barracks and told Paul. And Paul
called one of the centurions and said,
"Bring this young man to the tribune;
for he has something to tell him." So he
took him and brought him to the
tribune and said, "Paul the prisoner

called me and asked me to bring this
young man to you, as he has something
to say to you." The tribune took him
by the hand, and going aside asked him
privately, "What is it that you have to
tell me?" And he said, "The Jews have
agreed to ask you to bring Paul down to
the council tomorrow, as though they
were going to inquire somewhat more
closely about him. But do not yield to
them; for more than forty of their men
lie in ambush for him, having bound
themselves by an oath neither to eat nor
drink till they have killed him; and now
they are ready, waiting for the promise
from you." So the tribune dismissed
the young man, charging him, "Tell no
one that you have informed me of this"
(Acts 23:16-22).

Notice that Paul knows nothing about the tribune's response. But that is all right; there is no
need for him to be concerned. The Lord Jesus is
watching over him, and he has his man in the
right place. The man happens to be Paul's
nephew, and "by accident," we might say, he is
right there. "Coincidentally" he is at the right
spot to overhear the plans being laid, and he
comes to the tribune with the story.

A Small Army

Then you see how the protection of God ex-
tends into an open, public display:

Then he called two of the centurions
and said, "At the third hour of the

> night get ready two hundred soldiers
> with seventy horsemen and two hun-
> dred spearsmen to go as far as
> Caesarea. Also provide mounts for
> Paul to ride, and bring him safely to
> Felix the governor" (Acts 23:23,24).

Two hundred soldiers, seventy horsemen, and
two hundred spearsmen—that is four hundred
seventy armed men to protect one Christian!
That is a small army, and no band of Jewish
zealots is going to attack any force like that.
When the plot was laid, God relied upon Paul's
relative, his nephew, to help him. If you will per-
mit a very bad pun, he was "relatively" safe. But
now Paul is absolutely secure in the midst of this
force as he goes down to the coastline.

Letter of Acquittal

Now notice the preparation for Paul's appearance before the governor—again part of the protection of the Lord, provided by the letter that
the tribune wrote:

> And he wrote a letter to this effect:
> "Claudius Lysias to his Excellency the
> governor Felix, greeting. This man was
> seized by the Jews, and was about to be
> killed by them, when I came upon them
> with the soldiers and rescued him, hav-
> ing learned that he was a Roman
> citizen. And desiring to know the
> charge on which they accused him, I
> brought him down to their council. I
> found that he was accused about ques-
> tions of their law, but charged with

nothing deserving death or imprisonment. And when it was disclosed to me
that there would be a plot against the
man, I sent him to you at once, order-
ing his accusers also to state before you
what they have against him" (Acts
23:25-30).

It is obvious that this letter was designed to
make the tribune look as good as possible in the
eyes of the governor. He handles the truth rather
loosely. He implies that he rescued Paul because
he learned that he was a Roman citizen. This
would certainly look good on his record. But actually, as we know, he rescued him before he
was in danger, and then learned that he was a
citizen just before he was about to scourge him
unlawfully. But he did not put that detail in; this
is a politician's letter.

But it is also virtually a letter of acquittal of
any serious charge against the apostle. The gar-
rison commander goes on record in black and
white that as far as he can determine Paul has
done nothing that is worthy of death or even imprisonment. And so he prepares the way for Paul
to appear before the governor, laying the
groundwork for careful handling of this case.
This is evidence of that marvelous, amazing hand
of God, which can work through non-Christians,
nonbelievers, anyone, to accomplish His will and
purpose without their even being aware that
they are being used in any way. He simply works
through their normal reactions and feelings.

Finally we have Paul's presentation before the

governor:

> So the soliders, according to their instructions, took Paul and brought him by night to Antipatris. And on the morrow they returned to the barracks, leaving the horsemen to go on with him. When they came to Caesarea and delivered the letter to the governor, they presented Paul also before him. On reading the letter, he asked to what province he belonged. When he learned that he was from Cilicia he said, "I will hear you when your accusers arrive." And he commanded him to be guarded in Herod's praetorium (Acts 23:31-35).

It was sixty miles from Jerusalem to Caesarea. They covered the first forty by a rapid forced march. Fortunately it was downhill almost all the way. But nevertheless it was a hard night's march to travel the forty miles to the fortress of Antipatris. The next morning the horsemen brought Paul the remaining twenty miles to the governor's palace in Caesarea.

Felix was Pilate's successor as governor of Judea. He had been in office several years now. When he reads the letter he is obviously affected by it and kindly disposed toward Paul. All he asks, literally, is, "What kind of province does he come from?"

There were two kinds of provinces in the Roman empire. There were those under the control of the Roman senate, and those which reported to the emperor—the imperial provinces. He learns that Paul is from Cilicia, which, like

Judea, is an imperial province under the direct control of the emperor himself, responsible to him. And so the steps are being laid, as God is operating behind the scenes to pave the way for bringing Paul and the emperor, Nero, face-to-face. God will accomplish it *his* way.

CHAPTER FOUR

THE DISCIPLINE
OF DELAY

Acts 24:1-27

Felix is an interesting character. From secular history we know that he had been governor of the province of Judea for five years by the time of the events recorded in this chapter, and that he had previously lived for two years in the city of Samaria. He knew something about the Jews and their nation.

Felix had been born a slave, but his brother Pallas happened somehow to become a favorite of the emperor in Rome. Through the influence of Pallas, Felix was freed from slavery and was somewhat later appointed governor of this province. He was the first slave in history to become governor of a Roman province.

Felix had been married by this time to three different princesses. The first one we know nothing about, except that she was a princess. His second wife was the granddaughter of Antony and Cleopatra, whose names have been made famous by Shakespeare and Hollywood. The third wife, Drusilla, appears with Felix in this account. She was a Jewess, the daughter of Herod Agrippa, the king who had put the Apostle James to death. She had been the wife of the king of Emesa, but Felix had seduced her and now she was living with him as his wife.

This man was completely unscrupulous. He was known to hire thugs to eliminate people—even friends—who happened to get in the way of his political ambitions. It is before such a judge that the Apostle Paul was to appear.

The first nine verses of chapter 24 set forth the charges that are leveled against this apostle. First Luke lists the participants on this occasion:

> And after five days the high priest Ananias came down [to Caesarea] with some elders and a spokesman, one Tertullus. They laid before the governor their case against Paul; and when he was called, Tertullus began to accuse him . . .(Acts 24;1,2a).

Luke is careful to record that the high priest himself is here, because Ananias had been so mortally offended by the apostle when Paul had unwittingly insulted him, not knowing that he was the high priest, that he is thirsting for revenge. With him comes a delegation of elders, probably representing both the Pharisees and the Sadducees, and also an officious little Latin lawyer named Tertullus. We know that he was short of stature because his name is the diminutive of Tertius. It means "little Tertius." Can't you see him in your imagination?—short, fat, and pompous, busily strutting around the courtroom, trying to establish the case.

The Charges

Luke gives us an eyewitness account; he captures the very atmosphere of this scene. He probably wrote the account from notes he took on the spot. Here is the introduction to Tertullus' speech:

> . . . Tertullus began to accuse him, saying:

> "Since through you we enjoy much peace, and since by your provision, most excellent Felix, reforms are introduced on behalf of this nation, in every way and everywhere we accept this with all gratitude. But, to detain you no further, I beg you in your kindness to hear us briefly" (Acts 24:2-4).

If you read between the lines you can see what is happening. The lawyer begins to praise the governor with fulsome flattery. He starts out in this flowery way: "O most excellent Felix, we know that all these great things are happening in our nation because of you. . . ." Both he and Felix know that this is a bald-faced lie. The governor evidently indicates his impatience, perhaps with a frown or gesture, so the lawyer suddenly changes his tactics. He says, "To detain you no further, I beg you in your kindness to hear us briefly." Then he gets down to the point and sets forth the charges against Paul:

> For we have found this man a pestilent fellow, an agitator among all the Jews throughout the world, and a ringleader of the sect of the Nazarenes. He even tried to profane the temple, but we seized him. By examining him yourself you

will be able to learn from him about
everything of which we accuse him. The
Jews also joined in the charge, affirm-
ing that all this was so (Acts 24:5-9).

Undoubtedly Luke has given us merely a brief
summary of what this man said. Yet it is clear
that he leveled three particular charges against
Paul, charges particularly designed to arrest the
Roman governor's attention and to arouse his
antipathy against the apostle.

The first charge was that Paul was a revolutionary pest, a troublemaker, stirring up difficulties and riots all through the Empire. this
lawyer knew that such an accusation would have
an effect, because the Romans had a farflung
empire to administer, and the one thing they
dared not tolerate was civil disorder. Any upris-
ing could be a spark that would light a fire which
would be very difficult to put out. The Romans
dealt with any troublemaker with a heavy hand.

Second, Paul was labeled a religious radical, a
ringleader of the sect of the Nazarenes. Of course
Felix, having been governor, had heard of the
Nazarenes. Furthermore, he knew that there
were a lot of false messiahs around who were
ready to catch this fanatically religious nation up
in a wave of enthusiasm which could spell
nothing but trouble for Rome. Remember that
this was just a few years before the destruction of
Jerusalem by the Roman armies under Titus.
And, as Jesus had predicted, a wave of false
messiahs had come on the scene, false christs,
who claimed to be the true one. Tertullus was im-

plying that Paul was one of these.

The third charge leveled against Paul was that he was a sacrilegious fanatic who had tried to profane the temple, to defile it by bringing in Gentiles. That again was something to which the Romans would pay attention. Do you remember when, a few years ago, an Australian in a frenzy of religious fanaticism set fire to the Aqsah Mosque in the temple area of Jerusalem? How the nations of the world trembled, lest that single act of desecration precipitate a holy war which would embroil the Middle East, and perhaps the whole world, in conflict! That temple area was just as sensitive in the days of Rome. The Romans knew that to the Jews it was such a sacred precinct that anything that happened to their temple was apt to inflame the entire nation.

So all these charges were particularly designed to be of intense concern to the Roman administration. And yet there was not a word of truth in them. The Jews who came along simply affirmed them, but they did not offer any proof; they couldn't.

The Defense

Now Luke gives us the apostle's masterful defense:

> And when the governor had motioned to him to speak, Paul replied:

> "Realizing that for many years you have been judge over this nation, I cheerfully make my defense" (Acts 24:10).

He begins, you see, with the only nice state-
ment an honest man could make about Felix.
"You've been governor here for a number of
years." That is about all he could say. "I know
you've been around a long time. You know this
nation, and I hope you'll listen to me." And he
proceeds from there. With that careful,
methodical logic which we have come to expect
from the apostle, he answers these charges one
by one.

To the first charge, that he was a revolutionary
troublemaker, Paul says,

> As you may ascertain, it is not more
> than twelve days since I went up to wor-
> ship at Jerusalem; and they did not find
> me disputing with anyone or stirring
> up a crowd, either in the temple or in
> the synagogues, or in the city. Neither
> can they prove to you what they now
> bring up against me (Acts 24:11-13).

Paul's arguments are simple: "First, I have
had no time to incite a riot. It is only twelve days
since I went up to Jerusalem, and I've been absent from the province for years before that. You
can't get a riot going in twelve days. Second, I
made absolutely no effort to do so. I've never
even been seen disputing with anybody, either in
the temple or in the synagogues or in the city.
I've made no attempt anywhere to stir up any
difficulty, to arouse a crowd or incite emotions
in any way. And third, no proof whatsoever has
been offered for any of the claims made against
me. You have merely the afirmations of these

Jews that I did these things. But no evidence has been advanced at all." And so he completely demolishes this charge, exposing its emptiness.

Next he moves to the charge of being a religious radical. To this he answers:

> But this I admit to you, that according to the Way, which they call a sect, I worship the God of our fathers, believing everything laid down by the law or written in the prophets, having a hope in God which these themselves accept, that there will be a resurrection of both the just and the unjust. So I always take pains to have a clear conscience toward God and toward men (Acts 24:14-16).

To the second charge he pleads guilty. *"But,"* he says, "I want to point out that though I am indeed a follower of this Way, a member of what they call a sect, nevertheless it is most interesting to note that this 'sect' accepts the law and the prophets, just as these members of the Sanhedrin do. Furthermore, it stresses the hope which the Old Testament teaches, that of the resurrection of the dead, both just and unjust, and many of these Jews standing here believe it just as I do. And third, it results in a conscientious life, a life lived in good conscience before God and man. Now what can be so wrong with that?" He continues, "I admit I'm a member of this 'sect,' but so what? It simply agrees with all that these people themselves affirm to be the truth. What violation of Roman law is involved in becoming a member of this Christian group?" And with that he again demolishes the accusation against him.

The third charge was that of profaning the temple. To this the apostle replies:

> Now after some years I came to bring to my nation alms and offerings. As I was doing this, they found me purified in the temple, without any crowd or tumult. But some Jews from Asia—they ought to be here before you and to make an accusation, if they have anything against me. Or else let these men themselves say what wrongdoing they found when I stood before the council, except this one thing which I cried out while standing among them, "With respect to the resurrection of the dead I am on trial before you this day" (Acts 24:17-21).

His argument is very simple. "Rather than defiling the temple," he said, "I was bringing gifts of money and offerings to my people." Remember the collection for the saints at Jerusalem that he had brought there from Macedonia? "And," he says, "I also went into the temple and I worshiped there, as any Jew should. That is where they found me. But I wasn't disturbing anyone or profaning the temple. I was fulfilling its purpose."

"Furthermore," he points out, "the men who accuse me are not even present here. Certain Jews from Asia are the ones who brought the charges against me, and they're not even here." He waxes a little indignant. Here you can see how careful Luke has been in recording this. Paul's syntax gets a little mixed up. He starts out talking about the Jews from Asia but loses the thread of his thought, and ends up simply pointing out that they ought to be there to make an accusation. He never completes his sentence.

Finally he sums it all up, saying, "The most that I have done, the very most that can be charged against me, is that when I stood before the Sanhedrin in Jerusalem I said something that divided them among themselves. I cried out to them, 'With respect to the resurrection of the dead I am on trial before you this day.' Now if that is wrong then that is what I am guilty of." You can see how marvelously and completely he has dismissed these unfounded charges against him. What a masterful defense this is, made in a relatively few words, and how unanswerable are his arguments. He completely exonerates himself before the governor.

Unaccountable Delay

There is no question but that at this point the apostle legally should be released. But he is not, and as we go on to see, a strange and almost unaccountable delay occurs. This is where the story reaches out to include us. This is an account of one of God's inscrutable delays, which often afflict us as well. We think that something we want to happen is just around the corner. Then as we move toward it we find that it seems to recede from us, eluding our grasp. Sometimes it takes us months or years to reach a point which we thought was imminent. These circumstances raise questions in our minds and hearts, as they did with the apostle. Here we begin to see God's discipline of delay. In the remaining section it is brought before us by Luke:

> But Felix, having a rather accurate knowledge of the Way, put them off, saying, "When Lysias the tribune comes down, I will decide your case." Then he gave orders to the centurion that he should be kept in custody but should have some liberty, and that none of his friends should be prevented from attending to his needs (Acts 24:22,23).

Felix really does not need to have Lysias come down, for he has already received a letter from him exonerating Paul. But Felix uses this as an excuse, in order to hear something more from the apostle. Felix's curiosity has been awakened, and, as Luke tells us, he had "a rather accurate knowledge of the Way." He knows something about Christianity and wants to hear more. So he retains Paul in custody, even though he has every legal reason to set him free.

Now do not blame Felix unduly, for he is being used as an instrument to carry out God's purposes with Paul. The first evidence of that is Paul's continuing opportunity for witness to the governor:

> After some days Felix came with his wife Drusilla, who was a Jewess; and he sent for Paul and heard him speak upon faith in Christ Jesus. And as he argued about justice and self-control

and future judgment, Felix was alarm-
ed and said, "Go away for the present;
when I have an opportunity I will summon you." At the same time he hoped
that money would be given him by
Paul. So he sent for him often and con-
versed with him (Acts 24:24-26).

Paul is under "house arrest," the term we
would use today, with access to friends and with
some liberty. But he is still in the custody of the
Romans and unable to go about freely. After a
few days the governor sends for him. You can see
the Spirit of God working in this man's life.

A Terrified Governor

Paul's message had a profound effect upon
Felix. As the governor listened he was literally
"terrified"; he trembled. He felt the impact of
the logic of the apostle's presentation. Paul reasoned with him of *righteousness* (not justice; the
word should be righteousness), of *self-control,*
and of *future judgment,* judgment to come.
When he finished, Felix trembled.

Let's take a good look at what Paul said, bas-
ing our discussion on Luke's summary. He
began, first, to talk to Felix about righteousness
—that is, about God's expectation of humanity,
his rightful demand upon us. Here he is dealing,
basically, with the purpose of life. Why are you
here? What has God put you into the world to
do? All through the Gospels you find Jesus constantly unveiling before men the purpose of
human life: it is to produce true manhood and

womanhood, the righteousness of God, the proper behavior expected of mankind. Men were designed to behave in love and understanding, with tolerance and forgiveness, with all the characteristics that we instinctively know belong to manhood and to womanhood.

But the problem is that man is behaving unrighteously. Ask anybody on the street, "What's the matter with life today? What do we lack?" Everyone will say, "It's because other people don't behave as they should." They seldom point to themselves; it is the fault of "other people." Everybody blames everyone else. That is the lack of righteousnesss! And Paul, with his keen perception of human life, laid all this before the governor.

Then he went on to talk about self-control. This word appears only one other time in Paul's letters—in the listing of the fruit of the Spirit in Galatians 5. If the Holy Spirit is in us, then he is producing the life of Christ in us, and we will be characterized by love, joy, peace, longsuffering, gentleness, goodness, faith, meekness, *self-control*. That is the word used here. So when Paul talked with Felix about self-control he was talking about the fruit of the Spirit, and of the provision which God makes to meet the demand for righteousness. In other words, God not only asks men to behave rightly, but he also gives the power to do so.

Hidden Secrets

Finally, Paul told Felix about the judgment to come. A time is coming when every life will be evaluated, when each human being without exception will suddenly find himself standing naked before God, with all his life laid out for everyone to see. Then the value of that life, or the lack of it, will be evident to all. That is the judgment to come.

Jesus spoke of a time to come when whatever is spoken in secret will be shouted from the housetops, and whatever is hidden will be revealed. All the secrets of the heart, and everything done in secret, will be openly displayed. Undoubtedly Paul pointed out to Felix that God is aware of the hearts of men. He does not merely read the outside. We seem to be content if we can fool people by the exterior of our lives. If we look all right to them, that satisfies us. But Paul laid before the governor the fact that he was dealing with a God who reads the heart.

I have often said to audiences, "Wouldn't it be interesting if we had a television camera which could record thoughts? Suppose that as you came in this morning the camera was working on you, and all the thoughts you have had running through your mind this last hour were recorded on videotape. What would you think if we announced a public screening of that tape?"

That is exactly what is coming someday for us all—a time when everyone will see the life of everyone else, exactly as it was, with nothing hidden, nothing covered over. Then the great question will be: "In the face of God's demand for righteousness, what did you do about the provision he made to grant it? What did you do with Jesus Christ?''

When Paul reasoned this way before the governor, he trembled. And well he might! It all came to him. The logic of it hit him right between the eyes. But his response was: "Go away for the present; when I have an opportunity, I will summon you." He procrastinated because he had a problem. The fact that he delayed Paul's release, and then sent for him and even brought his wife to hear him, indicates that this man had a hunger for God. But, Luke says, he also wanted money from Paul.

Jesus said, "Seek ye first the kingdom of God, and his righteousness, and all other things shall be added to you." But you can't put them on the same level of priority. You can't want God *and* money. That is what destroys men. That is what blinded this man so that he could not see the exceeding importance of this moment.

Think of it! Felix had one of the most unusual opportunities ever afforded a human being—to spend *hours* with the Apostle Paul, to hear the clarity of his revelation of the nature of reality, of the way things really are, and to understand the truth as it is in Jesus. But Felix passed it by, turned his back and walked away. "Go away," he said, "until I have a more convenient season, a better opportunity." Do you know anything sadder, more pathetic, than those words? And though Felix called Paul to him and talked with him often, he never trembled again. That is the danger that men face when they are confronted with the reality of Jesus Christ and do nothing about it: their hearts are hardened.

The last sentence sums it all up for us:

> But when two years had elapsed, Felix was succeeded by Porcius Festus; and desiring to do the Jews a favor, Felix left Paul in prison (Acts 24:27).

There was absolutely no legal reason for this delay; it was only political expediency. Felix desired to do the Jews a favor, but it wasn't because of his love for them. Rather, as history tells us, he went too far once too often. We know from other records that at this time there was a clash in Caesarea between the Jews and the Greeks who lived there over the question of whether Caesarea was a Jewish or a Gentile city. The Jews won the encounter, and Felix therefore sent in troops to aid the Greeks. These Roman soldiers fell upon the Jews, killed thousands of them, looted the homes of the Jewish leaders, and burned them to the ground. As a result, the Jews complained to Nero, and Felix was relieved as governor and summoned back to Rome to answer for his conduct. He prepared for this as best he could, and, in order to retain as much favor among the Jews as possible, he left Paul in prison.

A Time to Learn

That was a tough situation for Paul to accept. Here is the apostle, eager to get on with his ministry, and yet he is in jail through no fault of his own. Legally, he ought to have been set free. But remember that Paul had chosen this course, and God is simply fulfilling that choice. Now Paul must accept delay in the fulfillment of his hope to get to Rome.

Yet God's delays are always times of learning. Though we are not told any more about what happened to the apostle here, we can nevertheless surmise that out of this time came many of the great truths which are reflected in Paul's letters. His letters to the Ephesians, to the Colossians, to the Philippians, and to Philemon were all written after this time. And in Philippians there is a passage which I think grew out of this situation. In the fourth chapter the apostle says,

> Not that I complain of want; for *I have learned,* in whatever state I am, to be content. I know how to be abased, and I know how to abound; in any and all circumstances *I have learned* the secrets of facing plenty and hunger, abundance and want. I can do all things in him who strengthens me (Philippians 4:11-13).

That is what you learn in a time of waiting. Dr. F.B. Meyer has written these words:

> So often we mistake God, and interpret his delays as denials. What a chapter might be written of God's delays. It is the mystery of the art of educating human spirits to the finest temper of which they are capable. What searchings of heart, what analyzings of motives, what testings of the Word of

God, what upliftings of the soul,
"searching what, or what manner of
time the Spirit of God signified." All
these are associated with these weary
days of waiting which are, nevertheless,
big with spritual destiny. But such delays
are not God's final answer to the soul
that trusts him.

Are you in prison right now? Do you find
yourself locked into circumstances which you are
helpless to change? Are you, by your own folly
perhaps, in a situation you cannot get out of? It
may be ill health, or a bad job. It may be a poor
marriage, or low finances, or something else.
Remember, God has given that to you in order
that you might learn the secret which Paul learned: "I can do all things in him who strengthens
me."

CHAPTER FIVE

THE GOSPEL AND KING AGRIPPA

Acts 25 & 26

The Apostle Paul is about to fulfill the great prediction which Jesus himself made about him when he called him to be an apostle. The Lord had said to Ananias, whom he had sent to Paul to pray with him and welcome him into the Christian family, "[This man is] a chosen instrument of mine to carry my name before the Gentiles and kings and the sons of Israel" (Acts 9:15). In Acts chapters 25 and 26, we will see that prophecy fulfilled.

First Paul appears before another pagan Roman governor. This part of the story serves as an introduction to Paul's appearance before King Agrippa, Luke's major focus in this section.

> Now when Festus had come into his province, after three days he went up to Jerusalem from Caesarea. And the chief priests and the principal men of the Jews informed him against Paul; and they urged him, asking as a favor to have the man sent to Jerusalem, planning an ambush to kill him on the way. Festus replied that Paul was being kept at Caesarea, and that he himself intended to go there shortly. "So," said

> he, "let the men of authority among
> you go down with me, and if there is
> anything wrong about the man, let
> them accuse him" (Acts 25:1-5).

We do not know much about Porcius Festus
from secular history, except that most historians
record him as a just man. But it is noteworthy
that the Jewish authorities waste no time when
Festus takes office. They immediately meet with
him and propose that he bring Paul up to Jerusalem, laying a plot to assassinate him on the
way. It seems almost as if this is where we came
in, does it not? That is exactly what was happening when Paul was taken down from Jerusalem
to Caesarea, back in chapter 23.

I have often wondered what happened to those
forty men who vowed, some 2½ years earlier,
neither to eat nor drink until they had killed
Paul. Either the ranks of Paul's enemies were
reduced considerably, or they found some
sneaky way to get out of their vow! I suppose the
latter is true, for they are probably among this
group who again plot to ambush Paul.

The Same Old Charges

But Festus is a Roman, and he is determined to
carry out Roman justice. So he refuses to bring
Paul up without at least having had a chance to
talk with the prisoner himself. Luke now tells us
about that hearing:

> When he had stayed among them not
> more than eight or ten days, he went
> down to Caesarea; and the next day he
> took his seat on the tribunal and

ordered Paul to be brought. And when he had come, the Jews who had gone down from Jerusalem stood about him, bringing against him many serious charges which they could not prove. Paul said in his defense, "Neither against the law of the Jews, nor against the temple, nor against Caesar have I offended at all." But Festus, wishing to do the Jews a favor, said to Paul, "Do you wish to go up to Jerusalem, and there be tried on these charges before me?" But Paul said, "I am standing before Caesar's tribunal, where I ought to be tried; to the Jews I have done no wrong, as you know very well. If then I am a wrongdoer, and have committed anything for which I deserve to die, I do not seek to escape death; but if there is nothing in their charges against me, no one can give me up to them. I appeal to Caesar." Then Festus, when he had conferred with his council, answered, "You have appealed to Caesar; to Caesar you shall go" (Acts 25:6-12).

Luke obviously gives us a very condensed description of this second trial. Evidently the arguments were all the same, the charges as unfounded as in the original trial, and Luke simply gathers it all up in two brief sentences.

But still that politician's phrase creeps in here, not only with Felix but with Festus as well: "wishing to do the Jews a favor. . . ." It is evident that Paul had become a political pawn, bandied about for political purposes between two ideologically divided parties.

Surely Paul has been hoping, all through these two long, weary years, that God would open the door to set him free. Yet he could not help but remember the Holy Spirit's words about what would happen if he went up to Jerusalem. Here we see the faithfulness of God in carrying out this limitation. Even though the apostle's heart and soul is one with the Lord once again, and there is nothing blocking the power of his ministry, nevertheless that ministry must be exercised only within the limitation of this otherwise-inexplicable inability to secure his freedom.

But now, I suspect, Paul is fed up with provincial justice. He knows that he will never stand a chance for justice in Jerusalem at the hands of the Jews. Nor has he ever forgotten that the Lord Jesus had appeared to him and told him he would go to Rome. So at last, reluctantly I think, Paul says, "I appeal to Caesar." Perhaps he felt that this would be the way God would work out his promise to bring him to Rome. Festus has no choice, according to Roman law, but to send him there to the emperor. Thus the fine hand of God is visible in the background of these events, carrying out his purposes. Paul is going to go to Rome, and God will take him there.

At this point an interesting development occurs. A Jewish king comes onto the scene:

> Now when some days had passed, Agrippa the king and Bernice arrived at Caesarea to welcome Festus. And as

they stayed there many days, Festus laid Paul's case before the king, saying,"There is a man left prisoner by Felix; and when I was at Jerusalem, the chief priests and the elders of the Jews gave information about him, asking for sentence against him. I answered them that it was not the custom of the Romans to give up anyone before the accused met the accusers face-to-face, and had opportunity to make his defense concerning the charge laid against him. When therefore they came together here, I made no delay, but on the next day took my seat on the tribunal and ordered the man to be brought in. When the accusers stood up, they brought no charge in his case of such evils as I supposed . . ." (Acts 25:13-18).

You can see that the Roman governor is troubled here. He thought that certain political charges would be leveled against Paul, since he was a political prisoner. But the accusations were of an entirely different nature. As he says,

". . . but they had certain points of dispute with him about their own superstition and about one Jesus, who was dead, but whom Paul asserted to be alive. Being at a loss how to investigate these questions, I asked whether he wished to go to Jerusalem and be tried there regarding them. But when Paul had appealed to be kept in custody for the decision of the emperor, I commanded him to be held until I could send him to Caesar." And Agrippa said to Festus, "I should like to hear the man myself." "Tomorrow," said he, "you shall hear him" (Acts 25:19-22).

Entertainment for the King

Thus the foundation is laid for Paul to appear before King Agrippa. We must realize, as we read this account, that this is not really another trial. It is more like an entertainment planned for Agrippa and Bernice. They had come to pay their respects to the Roman governor, to visit him at his capital city of Caesarea. It was the custom in those days, whenever a king arrived, to drum up a great deal of pomp, ceremony, and entertainment. In that spirit, Festus arranged to bring Paul before the king. The Roman governor, knowing Agrippa's religious background, suspected that he would be intrigued by the apostle's case.

King Agrippa was the last of the Herods. The Herodian kings belonged to the Jewish faith, although they were not exactly Jews, but Edomites, descendants of Esau, the twin brother of Jacob. The first of the line was Herod the Great, who killed the babies in Bethlehem when our Lord was born, in an attempt to slay the Messiah, whom he regarded as a rival to his throne. His son, Herod Antipas, had John the Baptist beheaded in prison. His grandson, Herod Agrippa I, put the Apostle James to death with the sword. Now his great-grandson, Agrippa II, has been appointed the high priest in Jerusalem, and to administer the temple. He was a Roman vassal, but all Jewish and Roman historians agree that he was a man of great mental acumen, expert in the affairs of the Jews.

With him was his wife Bernice. She was the sister of Drusilla, the wife of the previous Roman governor, Felix, and was also her own husband's sister. Agrippa and Bernice were full brother and sister! And yet, contrary to every law of the Jews, they were living in incest together as man and wife. It is before this morally profligate couple, enslaved by their own lust and passion, that the Apostle Paul is to appear—the enthroned prisoner appearing before the enslaved king.

Last Chance

As Luke goes on to paint this highly dramatic scene for us, we will see that there is a dawning hunger in Paul's heart to reach this king for Christ, despite his dark past. This is Paul's last chance to reach Israel, and he hopes against hope that perhaps the king will turn, so that the nation might follow.

> So on the morrow Agrippa and Bernice came with great pomp, and they entered the audience hall with the military tribunes and the prominent men of the city. Then by command of Festus Paul was brought in. And Festus said, "King Agrippa and all who are present with us, you see this man about whom the whole Jewish people petitioned me, both at Jerusalem and here,

> shouting that he ought not to live any longer. But I found that he had done nothing deserving death; and as he himself appealed to the emperor, I decided to send him. But I have nothing definite to write to my lord about him. Therefore I have brought him before you, and especially before you, King Agrippa, that after we have examined him, I may have something to write. For it seems to me unreasonable, in sending a prisoner, not to indicate the charges against him" (Acts 25:23-27).

Paul continually puzzled these Roman officials. Festus is particularly on the spot here because, by Roman law, he has the responsibility of sending Paul to the emperor to answer for charges. But he does not know what to write, for all the political charges have long since been disproved, as Paul has recently reminded him: "You know very well that I have done nothing against the Jews." And yet he has to say something, because if he sends a prisoner without a charge he himself will be criticized for governing ineptly. So he has elicited the aid of King Agrippa to find something that will hold water before the emperor.

Now Paul is brought in, chained to a Roman guard, and given the opportunity to make his defense:

> Agrippa said to Paul, "You have permission to speak for yourself." Then Paul stretched out his hand and made his defense: "I think myself fortunate

that it is before you, King Agrippa, I am to make my defense today against all the accusations of the Jews, because you are especially familiar with all customs and controversies of the Jews; therefore I beg you to listen to me patiently.

"My manner of life from my youth, spent from the beginning among my own nation and at Jeruslaem, is known by all the Jews. They have known for a long time, if they are willing to testify, that according to the strictest party of our religion I have lived as a Pharisee. And now I stand here on trial for hope in the promise made by God to our fathers, to which our twelve tribes hope to attain, as they earnestly worship night and day. And for this hope I am accused by Jews, O king! Why is it thought incredible by any of you that God raises the dead?

I myself was convinced that I ought to do many things in opposing the name of Jesus of Nazareth. And I did so in Jerusalem; I not only shut up many of the saints in prison, by authority from the chief priests, but when they were put to death I cast my vote against them. And I punished them often in all the synagogues and tried to make them blaspheme; and in raging fury against them, I persecuted them even to foreign cities" (Acts 26:1-11).

The substance of the apostle's argument

before King Agrippa is that he stands condemned because he was a good Jew. He is trying to appeal to the Jewish background and the Jewish sympathies of this king, in order to help him understand that there are no grounds of accusation against him and to use this as a way of reaching the soul of the king himself. Notice how neatly he does it.

First he points out that even the Jews present could testify to his Pharisaic background, to the fact that he was raised according to the strictest sect of the Jews. And second, he states that he believes nothing now, basically, that he did not believe then. He has not changed his faith at all—he is still a good Jew. He points out that the Jews were looking for the Messiah—that is the "promise made by God to our fathers"—and so was he.

Furthermore, the Jews believe in a resurrection. "And for this hope," he says, "I am accused by Jews, O king!" And then, addressing himself to the whole court, he says, "Why is it thought incredible by any of you that God raises the dead?" That is a good question! Certainly a Jew should not think it incredible, because God had said he would do this. Even Gentiles should hardly question the power of a Creator who brought forth life in the beginning to restore it if he wants to. It is perfectly unreasonable for man to think of raising the dead. Nobody has ever been able to achieve that. But it surely ought not to be unreasonable to expect God to be able to do so. You see how earnestly he is trying to appeal to the intelligence, the reationality, and the Jewish understanding of this king.

His third argument is that he demonstrated how sincere he was in his commitment to his beliefs by the way he persecuted the church. All this is to show Agrippa that he is a true Jewish believer in every sense of the word, that basically he has changed none of his fundamental beliefs, except with regard to the character of the Christians that he persecuted. The only thing that he concedes was wrong is that he was persecuting people whom he ought not to have persecuted.

The Citadel Assaulted

Now he marshals his forces and moves on to assault the citadel of Agrippa's will by telling him about his own conversion:

> "Thus I journeyed to Damascus with the authority and commission of the chief priests. At midday, O king, I saw on the way a light from heaven, brighter than the sun, shining round me and those who journeyed with me. And when we had all fallen to the ground, I heard a voice saying to me in the Hebrew language, 'Saul, Saul, why do you persecute me? It hurts you to kick against the goads' " (Acts 26:12-14).

Goads were sharp spikes often mounted on the front of chariots. If a horse kicked back he would hurt himself against them. The Lord said, "That is what is happening to you, Paul. You're kicking against the spikes, resisting the moving of the Holy Spirit." Paul continues,

"And I said, 'Who are you, Lord?'
And the Lord said, 'I am Jesus whom
you are persecuting. But rise and stand
upon your feet; for I have appeared to
you for this purpose, to appoint you to
serve and bear witness to the things in
which you have seen me and to those in
which I will appear to you, delivering
you from the people [the Israelites] and
from the Gentiles—to whom I send you
to open their eyes, that they may turn
from darkness to light and from the
power of Satan to God, that they may
receive forgiveness of sins and a place
among those who are sanctified by faith
in me' " (Acts 26:15-18).

Here is the heart of Paul's message—his own
transforming experience with Jesus Christ.
Notice that in verse 18 he lays the Good News out
before the king in a nutshell. What a marvelous
declaration of the gospel! Here from the words
of Jesus himself, as Paul recalls hearing them on
the Damascus road, is an accurate analysis of the
problem with humanity. Here is his description
of humanity in its lost, broken, fragmented condition. What is the matter with people? "They
are blind," Jesus says, "blind and living in darkness."

And then the Lord Jesus analyzes why men are
blind. "Because," he says, "they are under the
power of Satan." Behind the darkness is the
great enemy of mankind, who is twisting and distorting the thinking of men, clouding their eyes,
and spreading abroad widespread delusions. He

has loosed into this world a great flood of lying propaganda. And everywhere today men and women have believed these delusions and lies.

You hear them on every side. All the commonly accepted philosophies of our day reflect the basic satanic lie that we are capable, adequate, and independent—able to run our own affairs. You also hear that if you live for yourself, take care of "number one," you will find advancement and fulfillment in life. And you hear that material things can satisfy you, that if you get enough money you will be happy. All these lies permeate our society. That is the power and blindness of Satan.

But the power of the gospel is to turn men from darkness to light, and from the power of Satan to the power of God. The gospel is the good news that God has found a way to forgive men's sins, to wipe out all guilt from the mistakes of the past, from all that they have done in their ignorance and enslavement to the lying propaganda of Satan, and to give them a resource from which they may live in fulfillment and strength. That is what Jesus means by "an inheritance among those who are sanctified." And how do you get this? Jesus says precisely: "By faith in me."

This is why Christians insist that it is only through Jesus that men must find God. Why can't they find him through Buddhism, or Hinduism, or Mohammedanism, or some of the other great religions of the earth? Why aren't these equally acceptable? Their adherents are devout, sincere, religious people. Why do Christians insistently maintain that Jesus is the only way?

Jesus Says So

The answer is, that is what Jesus himself says. If we are to be Christians, we must follow him. We believe that he knows what he's talking about. We believe it because he has demonstrated that he understands life better than anyone else who has ever lived. The supreme proof of the fact is that he rose from the dead. He has solved the problem of death. He has unscrambled the great riddle with which we constantly struggle, this mystery of death. And, until I find someone else who has solved that problem and who has those credentials, I personally am going to follow Jesus.

If we are Christians, we believe him when he says, "I am the way, the truth, and the life; no man can come unto the Father but by me." We Christians have no other choice, because it was Jesus himself who said that all this happens "by faith in me." And of course, through the course of the centuries, wherever men have turned to him, they have indeed turned from darkness to light, and from the power of Satan to the power of God.

Now the apostle continues by stating that his ministry consisted in declaring this great liberating truth, but that thereby he has evoked the wrath of the Jews and they have tried to kill him for this reason. He also stresses again the two esential facts of the gospel—the death and the resurrection of Jesus Christ:

> "Wherefore, O King Agrippa, I was not disobedient to the heavenly vision, but declared first to those at Damascus, then at Jerusalem and throughout all the country of Judea, and also to the Gentiles, that they should repent and turn to God and perform deeds worthy of their repentance. For this reason the Jews seized me in the temple and tried to kill me. To this day I have had the help that comes from God, and so I stand here testifying both to small and great, saying nothing but what the prophets and Moses said would come to pass: that the Christ must suffer, and that, by being the first to rise from the dead, he would proclaim light both to the people and to the Gentiles" (Acts 26:19-23).

The Sober Truth

At this point there is an interruption. We read,

> And as he thus made his defense, Festus said with a loud voice, "Paul, you are mad; your great learning is turning you mad." But Paul said, "I am not mad, most excellent Festus, but I am speaking the sober truth. For the king knows about these things, and to him I speak freely; for I am persuaded that none of these things has escaped his notice, for this was not done in a corner. King Agrippa, do you believe the prophets? I know that you believe." And Agrippa said to Paul, "In a short time you think

to make me a Christian!" And Paul said, "Whether short or long, I would to God that not only you but also all who hear me this day might become such as I am—except for these chains."

Then the king rose, and the governor and Bernice and those who were sitting with them; and when they had withdrawn, they said to one another, "This man is doing nothing to deserve death or imprisonment." And Agrippa said to Festus, "This man could have been set free if he had not appealed to Caesar" (Acts 26:24-32).

Isn't it remarkable that Paul seldom ever got to finish a sermon? He was usually interrupted. In this case, Festus the skeptic, Festus the rationalist, could not take it when Paul referred to the resurrection. This was more than his Roman materialism could stand, so he said, "Paul, you're mad, you're crazy! Talking about raising the dead!" But Paul answered, "Most excellent Festus, I am telling you the cold, sober truth. That is what Christianity is all about. That is the tremendous, stupendous declaration which is at the heart of Christianity! Christ has solved the problem of death! It seems absolutely incredible, perhaps, but it is true! God has broken through death and in Jesus Christ he has made life available to men once again, as God intended life to be."

Then he turns and looks at Agrippa. You can see that he is longing to reach this man, for this is his last chance, and he knows it, to reach the

Jewish people as a whole. He says, "I am persuaded that none of these things have escaped King Agrippa's notice, for this was not done in a corner." That is, "Everything is open, nothing is hidden. The Lord preached and taught, lived and died, right out in the open before everyone, and I know the king knows the story."

And then, speaking directly to Agrippa, he says, "King Agrippa, do you believe the prophets? I know that you believe." He is saying, "You know the historical facts of Jesus' life. And you believe the prophets. So put the two together. What did the prophets say the Messiah would do? Where does that lead you? Jesus fulfilled what the prophets wrote."

At this point this enslaved king, mastered by his own lusts, living with his own sister, is faced right into the issue. You can see him squirming there on his seat. Unfortunately, his answer is to turn his back on what Paul says.

It is a little difficult to understand exactly what he replied, because the Greek is a bit obscure. Certainly he did not say what we have in our King James Version: "Almost thou persuadest me to be a Christian." He is not saying, "You've almost got me, Paul. You almost have me convinced." Many a message has been preached on that theme, as though Agrippa had come to the point of becoming a Christian.

It is much more likely that he said what is recorded in the Revised Standard Version. With almost sneering sarcasm he says, "Do you really think, Paul, that in this short a time you're going to make me a Christian? You've got to do a lot more than that if you're going to make *me* a Christian.''

But Paul's reply is magnificent. With a heavy heart he says, "King Agrippa, whether I had to spend a short time or a long time with you, I just want you to know that the hunger of my heart is that not only you, on your throne with your wife beside you, but that everyone in this room could be like I am—except for these chains.''

Paul's answer is hardly that of a prisoner. As he stands there he says, "I wish you could be like I am. I wish you had the peace, the liberty, the power, the joy, the gladness of my heart and life.'' What an appeal out of a great heart! What a revelation of the greatness of the gospel! It can rise above every circumstance, every situation, and fill the heart with joy.

But remember that Agrippa is a Herod. He is an Edomite, a descendant of Esau, and he is true to his heritage. God had said through the prophet Malachi, "Jacob have I loved, but Esau have I hated.'' Esau stands throughout Scripture as a mark of that independent spirit which refuses help from God. It turns its back upon all the love of God poured out to reach us, and in independent arrogance refuses the proffered hand of God's grace. That is what this king does. So now he fades from history; he is the last of the line of the Herods.

But Paul's great words ring in our ears down through the centuries. There is nothing like the liberty of Jesus Christ. No external condition of wealth or prestige or power is worth a snap of a finger compared with the freedom and power and joy and gladness that a man can find in Jesus Christ.

CHAPTER SIX

GOD AND SHIPWRECKS

Acts 27

If you are a sailor or lover of the sea, I know you will be particularly interested in this passage. Acts 27 is a fascinating account of Paul's voyage to Rome and of the shipwreck that occurred on the way. Luke was not a sailor; he was a landsman, and yet he was such a careful historian that the details he gives in this chapter about ancient methods of sailing afford more insight into sailing practices on the Mediterranean in the first century than all other ancient manuscripts put together.

The chapter divides itself readily into four major movements. The first one reads almost like a page out of a ship's log. It gives us the list of the important passengers on this voyage and also explains some of the problems they faced as they began to sail from Caesarea to Rome. Thus the story begins on a note which is characteristic of the entire voyage. There are difficulties and delays all the way through.

Paul is now on his way to Rome to appear before the emperor, Nero. Paul is still a prisoner, still in the custody of the military, still chained for much of the time to a Roman guard. Luke tells us:

> And when it was decided that we should sail for Italy, they deliverd Paul and some other prisoners to a centurion of

> the Augustan Cohort, named Julius.
> And embarking in a ship of Adra-
> myttium, which was about to sail to the
> ports along the coast of Asia, we put to
> sea, accompanied by Aristarchus, a
> Macedonian from Thessalonica. The
> next day we put in at Sidon; and Julius
> treated Paul kindly, and gave him leave
> to go to his friends and be cared for
> (Acts 27:1-3).

Here are the major personalities we will meet
in this chapter. Paul, of course, is central in all of
the latter portion of Acts. He is delivered to the
charge of a centurion named Julius, whom we
have not met previously. Julius appears to be a
very kindhearted individual who treats Paul with
great courtesy and respect throughout this voyage. He
obviously does not regard Paul as a common
criminal but as a political prisoner worthy of
consideration.

The centurion belonged to the Augustan
Cohort of the Roman military establishment.
This was a very prestigious unit, a picked body of
soldiers responsible directly to the emperor
himself. As such, the centurion had considerable
authority. With them traveled Dr. Luke, who as
Paul's personal physician was permitted to go
along. Many scholars have felt that this fact confirms the theory that the apostle was suffering
from physical difficulty and needed a physician
with him.

The other person Luke mentions is Aristarchus, a young man whom Paul had met in
Thessalonica on his second missionary journey

and who now faithfully accompanies the apostle wherever he goes. The interesting thing about his presence here is that because Paul was a prisoner it was necessary, most scholars feel, for Aristarchus to be Paul's slave in order to accompany him on this voyage. So great was his love for Paul and so strong was his desire to minister to his needs that he volunteered to serve in that capacity.

Against the Wind

Their little vessel is beating its way up the coast of Palestine toward what we call Aisa Minor, or Turkey. The voyage continues as they sail from Sidon:

> And putting to sea from there we sailed under the lee of Cyprus, because the winds were against us. And when we had sailed across the sea which is off Cilicia and Pamphylia, we came to Myra in Lycia. There the centurion found a ship of Alexandria sailing for Italy, and put us on board. We sailed slowly for a number of days, and arrived with difficulty off Cnidus, and as the wind did not allow us to go on, we sailed under the lee of Crete off Salmone. Coasting along it with difficulty, we came to a place called Fair Havens, near which was the city of Lasea (Acts 27:4-8)

At this particular time of year the winds usually blew from the northeast, which would have helped them on their way to Rome. But for some reason this time they met nothing but a constant, strong northwest wind, making it necessary for them to duck behind the island of Cypress and to hug the Asian coast, tacking against the wind.

They finally arrive at the Lycian port of Myra, where they find a much larger vessel, probably 120 feet long or more—fairly large even by modern standards. This was a grain ship carrying wheat from Egypt, the granary of the Roman Empire. Driven also by the contrary winds, it had been forced to put into port here on this coast. The centurion evidently leases the vessel, because he is in charge of it for the rest of th voyage.

But once again they run into contrary winds, and with great difficulty they make slow progress, having to tack back and forth, zigzagging in their course. After several days of sailing they have come only a couple hundred miles and must slide down under the lee of the island of Crete in order to make any headway at all.

The difficulty they met raises a question which becomes increasingly pertinent as we go through this chapter: why would the apostle experience such grave difficulty from natural forces when he is obviously in the center of the will of God, on the way to Rome, where the Lord wants him to be? Paul is not being disobedient; he is moving right in God's purpose. Nevertheless, the winds are contrary and everthing else seems to go wrong on this voyage. God, who controls the winds and the waves, could surely have made it easy for Paul to get to Rome. We all face this question from time to time. Even when we are doing what we take to be God's will for us, why do we often still have such great difficulty in accomplishing it?

We will face the implications of that before we get to the end of the chapter, but there is still a lot more difficulty ahead.

The second major movement takes us through verse 20 and tells us of the divisions and dangers that they encounter on the voyage:

> As much time had been lost, and the voyage was already dangerous because the fast had already gone by, Paul advised them, saying, "Sirs, I perceive that the voyage will be with injury and much loss, not only of the cargo and the ship, but also of our lives." But the centurion paid more attention to the captain and to the owner of the ship than to what Paul said. And because the harbor was not suitable to winter in, the majority advised to put to sea from there, on the chance that somehow they could reach Phoenix, a harbor of Crete, looking northeast and southeast, and winter there (Acts 27:9-12).

You notice that even though Paul is a prisoner he is given considerable freedom. In fact, when he gives some advice about the voyage he is heard very courteously. His counsel is based not upon an exercise of the gift of prophecy but simply upon basic common sense. He says that it is too late in the year to try to make it to Rome. The fast he mentions is the great fast on the Day of Atonement of the Jews, which means that it is early October. They are soon to face the blast of late fall and winter, when sailing on the Mediterranean is very dangerous indeed. Sudden storms can rise without warning and can sometimes last for days. Paul, knowing this, advises that they winter in the little port where they are.

A Boring Place

But he is met immediately with a difference of opinion. The captain and the owner of the ship, as well as the majority of the crew, differ with him. Luke is careful to record the reason why. They had taken one look around at the dinky little town of Fair Haven and had decided that this was a boring place to spend a winter. They would have no way of amusing themselves, so they want to get out of there and into a more exciting place. They obviously have their own comfort and convenience at heart rather than the safety of the ship. So they prevail upon the centurion, who evidently has the last word, to head for the city of Phoenix, a harbor about fifty miles up the coast of Crete. But as the modern song reminds us, a lot of things can happen before you get to Phoenix. The next section brings us the account of the storm that arose:

> And when the south wind blew gently, supposing that they had obtained their purpose, they weighed anchor and sailed along Crete, close inshore. But soon a tempestuous wind, called the northeaster, struck down from the land; and when the ship was caught and could not face the wind, we gave way to it and were driven. And running under the lee of a small island called Cauda,

we managed with difficulty to secure
the boat; after hoisting it up, they took
measures to undergird the ship; then,
fearing that they should run on the Syrtis, they lowered the gear, and so were
driven. As we were violently storm-
tossed, they began next day to throw
the cargo overboard; and the third day
they cast out with their own hands the
tackle of the ship. And when neither
sun nor stars appeared for many a day,
and no small tempest lay on us, all hope
of our being saved was at last abandoned (Acts 27:13-20).

What a tremendous gale! And yet it had all
begun so encouragingly with the south wind
blowing softly. You can see that human nature
has not changed one bit. As soon as these sailors
found a fair day they immediately cast all cau-
tion to the winds and believed what they wanted
to believe. How many times we have been
similarly fooled by seemingly favorable circumstances.

They had no sooner sailed outside the limits of
the harbor than a tremendous tempest blew in, a
northeaster blowing away from the land, one of
the sudden storms that spring up in the late fall
on the Mediterranean even to this day. The
violence of the storm is underscored by Luke's
account. The wind was so strong right from the
beginning that they could not sail against it and
get back to the island even though they were still
close to shore. So they had to let the ship be
driven before the wind.

Then they had a hard time hoisting the lifeboat

into the ship. They didn't carry them aboard in those days, but pulled them behind until a storm came up. But the sea was so violent that they could not secure it. It was only when they ran under the lee of a small island and got out of the wind a bit that they were able to do so, and even then only with great difficulty. They even found it necessary to take cables and slide them under the ship and tie it up like a package in order to hold it together. The weight of the grain, shifting in the wildness of the storm, threatened to tear the ship apart, and without this undergirding they never would have survived as long as they did. Finally, Luke tells us, they lowered all the sails so that the wind would have as little purchase as possible, and in this way they tried to ride out the storm.

But they were still afraid that they would be driven onto the great sand banks called the Syrtis, which lined the coast of north Africa, where the ship would be marooned miles out from shore. This was one of the most feared hazards of sailing on the Mediterranean. As the storm increased in fury their despair began to grow. They threw overboard much of the cargo and then even the mainsail and its tackle.

They Gave Up Hope

As Luke tells us, "when neither sun nor stars appeared for many a day," they gave up hope. The absence of the sun and stars was a terrible handicap to them because these ancient navigators had no compass or any other instrument. The only way they could guide the ship was by the sun and stars. When they could not

see them for many days they lost all knowledge
of their whereabouts. They were driven helpless-
ly before a howling gale in the midst of a tur-
bulent sea with no idea where they were headed.
And so at last they gave up all hope of being
saved.

Luke's account suggests that even the Apostle
Paul gave up hope of surviving this voyage—at
least on this ship. Along with the rest of them he
despaired of avoiding shipwreck, although of
course he knew that he would get to Rome in
some way or other because God had promised
him that. But it was a perilous situation.

Again we must ask, Why all this difficulty
when the apostle is fulfilling the will of God? The
situation gets worse and worse as it goes along!
What is happening? Why do these discouraging
circumstances keep piling up? Well, the third
movement will answer this, at least in part. Here
we have the sudden interjection of encouragement and promise:

> As they had been long without food,
> Paul then came forward among them
> and said, "Men, you should have
> listened to me, and should not have set
> sail from Crete and incurred this injury
> and loss. I now bid you take heart; for
> there will be no loss of life among you,
> but only of the ship. For this very night
> there stood by me an angel of the God
> to whom I belong and whom I worship,
> and he said, 'Do not be afraid, Paul;
> you must stand before Caesar; and lo,
> God has granted you all those who sail
> with you.' So take heart, men, for I

> have faith in God that it will be exactly
> as I have been told. But we shall have to
> run on some island" (Acts 27:21-26).

Luke has taken note of the distress of these men. They had for many days been so upset and anxious over the outcome of this voyage that fear had destroyed their appetites and they had not eaten. In the midst of that, our version says, the apostle came forward. But in Greek the words are literally "he stood forth"—he stood out among them, with a different attitude and point of view.

A Startling Message

When Paul stands before these men and says, "You should have listened to me," he is not merely indulging in an "I told you so." He is trying to awaken them to the obvious evidence that what he had said before was right, and thus he is encouraging them to pay attention to what he says *now,* beause it is a very startling message. Despite all the contrary evidence around them on every side, Paul announced with absolute conviction, "There will be no loss of life among you, but only of the ship."

His reason for saying so, he says, is that an angel had come to him just the night before and had encouraged him with the message that he was going to stand before Caesar and that he was not to be afraid. This indicates that fear had begun to creep even into the apostle's heart. But he is reassured by the angelic messenger.

Furthermore the angel said, "God has granted you all those who sail with you." In the phrase

"God has granted you," you can see what Paul has been doing. He has been praying for these others, praying that the sailors and soldiers accompanying him would be spared as well as that his own object would be accomplished on this trip. God heard his prayer and granted him their lives.

This incident is given to us to show us the tremendous power that a man of faith exercises. I wish I could get this across to people today. I have a feeling that none of us, myself included, has any idea of the power God has committed to us in the instrument of prayer. He does mighty things if we will only ask him. Remember that James says, "You have not because you ask not." God stands ready to grant us *much* more than we have ever dreamed about.

The church is really the secret government of earth, for it has power to control the current events which happen around us, the events reported in our newspapers. We sometimes feel that we are only helpless pilgrims drifting through this age, waiting to get to heaven someday. But the Scriptures never portray a Christian that way. He is intimately related to the events happening around him, and he has great control over them.

That is why James also says, "The prayer of a righteous man [literally] *releases great power.*" Here God granted this one man, because of his prayer, the lives of the 275 individuals who sailed with him. They were spared because Paul prayed for them. What a revelation of the power of prayer!

Secret Help

Notice also the secret help given to the believer in time of distress. Paul was exposed to the same peril as these other men, and yet God strengthened him with a word of encouragement in the midst of the trial. He didn't take him away from it; the storm was no less severe for Paul than it was for anyone else. The danger was just as evident, the waves were just as high, the darkness was just as intense, the apparent hope was just as absent from the circumstances for him as it was for them. Everything was exactly the same except that God granted to Paul an encouraging word, a secret knowledge that the others did not possess. He did not lessen the pressure but he gave an inward reassurance that enabled Paul to stand out from the rest of them and be different.

That is what the Christian faith is all about. It is a way of discovering hidden resources, secret resources which others do not know about, which make it possible for you to live and act and react differently from those around you. That is the characteristic of Christianity; that is what it is supposed to be like all the time.

Some time ago I was at Fuller Theological Seminary and heard Mr. Bill Pannell, a black evangelist associated with Tom Skinner, speak at the chapel. He reminded us all that Christianity does not operate on the same principles upon which the world lives. He illustrated this by the remarkable event in our Lord's life which we call the "triumphal entry." This was the day during our Lord's last week when he entered Jerusalem. Mr. Pannell said that if he had been in charge it would have looked much more like the Rose Parade. He would have brought Jesus in on a white horse with a beautiful silver-mounted saddle, accompanied by a long retinue. And there would have been a band, perhaps even a Scottish bagpipe band, to go before him and introduce him.

But our Lord did not choose that kind of ceremony. His method was to ride into town on a jackass. He did it that way to illustrate that he operates on a totally different basis. The values which the world places upon something are rejected by God. Luke tells us in his Gospel that Jesus once said, "The things which are highly esteemed among men are an abomination in the sight of God."

The Christian lives by a different principle. In the midst of circumstances which would panic others, the Christian is expected to be calm. We are not to reflect the panic, the anxiety, and the troubled countenance which others display when they get into difficulty. As Rudyard Kipling describes it in his famous poem, "If you can keep your head when all about you men are losing theirs and blaming it on you . . ." then that is true manhood; a resource is granted to Christians which others know nothing about.

I am afraid that today too many Christians follow the modern version of that line: "If you can keep your head when others are losing theirs . . . you just don't understand the situation!" But Paul understood the situation, yet still kept his head and stood out among them, distinctive because of his faith. Notice his confident word: "So take heart, for I have faith in God that it will be exactly as I have been told." That is faith.

The remainder of the chapter gives us the story of the disaster that occurred and the deliverance which followed:

> When the fourteenth night had come, as we were drifting across the sea of Adria, about midnight the sailors suspected that they were nearing land. So they sounded and found twenty fathoms; a little farther on they sounded again and found fifteen fathoms. And fearing that we might run on the rocks, they let out four anchors from the stern, and prayed for day to come. And as the sailors were seeking to escape from the ship, and had lowered the boat into the sea, under pretense of laying out anchors from the bow, Paul said to the centurion and the soldiers, "Unless these men stay in the ship, you cannot be saved." Then the soldiers cut away the ropes of the boat, and let it go (Acts 27:27-32).

Things seem to get worse and worse as this story goes on. Not only do they face the terrible dangers of the storm, but as they drift on through the blackness of night they hear the frightening roar of breakers in the distance. They do not know where they are nor what kind of strange land they might be coming upon nor what kind of shore it will have. (We know today that they were approaching the island of Malta, but they did not know that.) As they hear the breakers pounding against the rocks they are afraid the ship will be broken to pieces and all their lives will be lost. So they cast out some anchors from the stern to slow the drift of the ship and pray that they will hold it offshore at least until daybreak, when they can see the kind of peril they are coming upon.

Then, to make matters worse, the sailors hatch a little plot to abandon ship and save their own skins, leaving the rest to get by as best they can. They decide that they will get into the boat, and, under the pretense of letting out more anchors, they will simply row ashore and leave the ship to its fate. We are not told how, but somehow (again, God's man in the right place at the right time) Paul learns of this plot and says to the centurion, "Unless these men stay in the ship, you cannot be saved." He knows that the ship cannot be beached properly unless the sailors who know how to handle it are there. And, military man that he is, the centurion acts promtply. He commands the soldiers to cut the rope and let the boat drift off. So they all remained in the same ship together.

Man's Activity Included

The interesting thing about this is that God had promised Paul that every life would be spared. Yet Paul could say to the centurion, "Unless these men stay in the ship, you will not be saved." God's promise includes man's activity. Man's actions are the means by which God works out his promises, for God's announced purpose never cancels out man's activity.

The fact that God announces the end result does not mean that men are permitted to fold their hands and say, "Well, it's all going to work out some way or another." He intends for us to exercise considerable understanding of a situation and to act in line with common sense in carrying out his purpose. Paul knows that he must work toward that end and that the decisions along the way are part of God's means of accomplishing it. So he insists that the sailors stay aboard the ship.

In the next section we read of still another danger:

> As day was about to dawn, Paul urged them all to take some food, saying, "Today is the fourteenth day that you have continued in suspense and without food, having taken nothing. Therefore I urge you to take some food; it will give you strength, since not a hair is to perish from the head of any of you." And when he had said this, he took bread, and giving thanks to God in the presence of all, he broke it and began to eat. Then they all were encouraged and ate some food themselves (We were in all two hundred and seventy-six persons in the ship.) And when they had eaten enough, they lightened the ship, throwing out the wheat into the sea (Acts 27:33-38).

Fourteen days without any food! That is quite a diet. It had reduced this ship's company to a state of physical weakness bordering on helplessness. We saw earlier that they had lost their appetite through fear. They were so frantic about their situation that they had no desire for food. Their physical condition was due to spiritual despair.

This is an interesting revelation of the tie between the physical and the spiritual within us. Because the physical weakness is due to spiritual despair, it is therefore a spiritual cure which permits them to eat. Paul reminds them of the promise of God. He encourages their faith, saying, "Not a hair is going to perish from the head of any of you." And, suiting actions to words, he takes bread himself, gives thanks, then breaks and eats it in front of them. This encourages them all to eat and strengthen their lives.

Here again is the action of the man of faith. In the midst of discouraging circumstances and discouraged people, he acts on a different basis than they. The result is that they are all encouraged. One man with hope in his heart and encouragement on his lips was able to change the attitude of 275 other people, so that they ate and were physically prepared for the rigors that lay immediately ahead. That again is the power of faith.

In the last section we see the final threats from nature and from man:

> Now when it was day, they did not recognize the land, but they noticed a bay with a beach, on which they planned if possible to bring the ship ashore. So they cast off the anchors and left them in the sea, at the same time loosening the ropes that tied the rud-

ders; then hoisting the foresail to the wind they made for the beach. But striking a shoal they ran the vessel aground; the bow stuck and remained immovable, and the stern was broken up by the surf. The soldiers' plan was to kill the prisoners, lest any should swim away and escape; but the centurion, wishing to save Paul, kept them from carrying out their purpose. He ordered those who could swim to throw themselves overboard first and make for the land, and the rest on planks or on pieces of the ship. And so it was that all escaped to land (Acts 27:39-44).

The bay that they saw when dawn finally came under the heavy skies is now called St. Paul's Bay on the island of Malta. They decided that it was there or nowhere, and that their only chance was to beach the ship in this little harbor. So they threw overboard everything that would hinder the ship from going in as far as possible, and, hoisting the foresail to the wind, they made for the beach.

But another natural obstacle looms when they run aground in a shallow area where two seas meet. The boat is stuck some distance from shore and begins to break up in the surf. They have to abandon ship and jump overboard, those who can swim going first, and the others making it on planks and other pieces of the ship.

But that still is not the last peril, especially to the prisoners, for the soldiers decide to kill them all. This is understandable in view of the Roman law, which said that any soldier who allowed a prisoner to escape was himself subjected to the same penalty the prisoner would have received. These soldiers were not willing to take that risk, and it was customary to kill prisoners if there was no longer any possibility of guarding them properly.

But once again it is Paul who indirectly saves the situation. The centurion—kindhearted, authoritative Julius—because he had come to respect Paul takes the entire responsibility upon himself, countermands the plans of the soldiers, and thus saves the lives of these prisoners, Paul included.

Finally, through the storm and the surf and everything else, they make their way to shore. And, as Paul had been told by God, not a single life is lost. Verse 44 reads almost as a sigh of relief at the end of this chapter: "And so it was that all escaped to the land." We can heave that sigh along with them.

Now we have to answer the question, Why do shipwrecks come to us in the midst of doing the will of God? Why is it that Christians face this kind of difficulty? I recently talked with a man who shared with me from his own experience the shipwreck that had occurred in his first marriage. He told me how he had begun it with deep high hopes and dreams and deep commitment to God for its success. And yet it had broken, foundered, and been shipwrecked. He shared with me how this tore him, how he did not know what to make of it, how it shattered his faith and challenged his concepts. What searchings of heart this brought to him! What painful re-evaluation it had meant! I could empathize with him as he unfolded to me the bitterness and resentment that stirred in his heart as he struggled with the question which all of us must face at times: "Why do these difficulties come when we are doing the right thing? We could understand it if they hit us when we were doing wrong, but why when we are doing right?"

Satanic Opposition

The Scriptures give several answers. First of all, these difficulties are clearly the result of satanic opposition. In Paul's letter to the Romans he said that he had tried many times to go to Rome and had been prevented, hindered. Paul always said it was Satan who had put those hindrances in his path. The enemy did not want Paul in Rome, for that was the strategic center of the empire and also the very headquarters of evil. Satan did not want this mighty apostle, coming in the strength and power of a risen Lord, to move into this city and start breaking down the strongholds of darkness by which Satan held in grip the entire civilized world. So Satan delayed Paul every way he could, fighting every step of the way. He sent the contrary winds, the storm, and all the other difficulties that this chapter recites for us.

And yet, having said that, it is also well to remember that God had permitted all this. God is greater and stronger than Satan. His might and power could have canceled out this opposition. He could have made the winds blow in the right direction. He could have said to Satan, "This far and no farther. Take your hands off. Stop this hindrance!" But he deliberately did not do it.

Again, Scripture suggests some reasons why

God sometimes does not intervene to prevent Satan's work. One is that there were lessons in this for the others who sailed with Paul. Imagine what they learned of a different way of life as they watched this man of faith in the midst of the same perils they were facing. His reaction was so different from theirs. There was a baffling element guiding and guarding this man, keeping him stable in the midst of these circumstances. Those watching were impressed by it. And how encouraging Paul could be, how reassuring he was to others. Again and again he was the man in the critical moment who saved the day. They owed their lives to him time and time again before the voyage was over. He showed them that there is a new way of life, different from that by which the world lives.

There were also lessons for Paul in this. He too grew in faith as he learned how faithful God could be and how he could move in so that things would go only so are, and then at the critical moment a line would be drawn. Paul tells us that God's strength is made perfect in man's weakness. "So," he says, "I glory in my infirmity." He grew to understand more about the love and grace of God as he went through these dangerous times.

Any Questions?

Finally, of course, the great story of the Book of Job shows us that even when there is seemingly no explanation at all, in terms of this life, for the shipwrecks and disasters which believers go through, there is still that unseen victory in realms far beyond the visible, which honors and glorifies God and makes possible great progress and advance in the kingdom of God. You remember that in the Book of Job, Satan and God and Job are all there at the beginning. But at the end there are just God and Job. And God says to Job, "I'm responsible for all of this. Do you have any questions?"

How are we ever going to understand what is happening to us unless we accept our circumstances in the light of the reality which Scripture reveals? As I read this account a verse of Scripture from the Psalms rings over and over in my mind. It is from Psalm 34, verse 19:

> Many are the afflictions of the righteous;
> but the Lord delivers him out of them all.

That is the story of life, isn't it? We must expect these shipwrecks. But the Lord delivers us out of them all. The next verse in that psalm is a prophecy of the crucifixion. It says of Jesus,

> He keeps all his bones;
> not one of them is broken.

Even through the disaster and shipwreck of the Cross, God's forestalling hand was there, allowing it to go only so far, limiting it, controlling it, permitting much darkness and disaster, agony and bloodshed, but nevertheless solidly in control, undergirding and carrying Jesus through. So, as we look at this story of the shipwreck of Paul, and at the voyage of life which all of us are taking, we have to say, as many of us have learned to say through the years, "Everything went wrong, but it all turned out right."

CHAPTER SEVEN

THE END OF
THE BEGINNING

Acts 28

We have arrived at the last page of the first chapter of church history—the last chapter of the Book of Acts. Luke's unfinished book introduces us to the whole record of the history of the church which continues to this day. In this chapter the suspenseful account of Paul's voyage to Rome continues:

> After we had escaped, we then learned that the island was called Malta. And the natives showed us unusual kindness, for they kindled a fire and welcomed us all, because it had begun to rain and was cold. Paul had gathered a bundle of sticks and put them on the fire, when a viper came out because of the heat and fastened on his hand. When the natives saw the creature hanging from his hand, they said to one another, "No doubt this man is a murderer. Though he has escaped from the sea, justice has not allowed him to live." He, however, shook off the creature into the fire and suffered no harm. They waited, expecting him to swell up or suddenly fall down dead; but when they had waited a long time and saw no misfortune come to him, they changed their minds and said that he was a god (Acts 28:1-6).

They spent some three months on Malta waiting for the winter to pass so that navigation could resume. The impressive thing about their stay is that it was a time characterized by healing. It began with this amazing healing of the apostle himself from the bite of a poisonous snake.

Notice that this event occurred in the midst of what we would call a rather primitive, uncivilized society. The word translated "natives" in our version is really the word "barbarians" in Greek. The Greeks called anybody who spoke in a tongue other than Greek a barbarian. That is because any other language sounded to them like a cacophony of sounds. They could distinguish no words. We have all had the experience of listening to a language utterly foreign to us and wondering how anybody can understand anything in it. It sounds to us like an unintelligible jumble of syllables. The Greeks thought the noises they made sounded like "bar-bar," or meaningless syllables. To them "bar-bar" was the mark of someone who had not yet learned to speak the civilized language, Greek, so they called them "barbarians."

But these were not naked savages. Primitive societies are often more complex and advanced in their own way than what we fondly (or unfondly) call civilization. These natives treated their guests with unusual kindness and courtesy. Literally, in Greek, it was "kindness more than ordinary." This indicates that the Holy Spirit was preparing the hearts of these barbarians, these pagans, to hear the gospel. Here was a people prepared to receive the message of God, disposed by the effect of the Spirit upon their hearts to be open and receptive.

That is almost always characteristic of paganism. Pagans are what C.S. Lewis calls "pre-Christians"; that is, they are very open to the gospel. They have been prepared for it by the emptiness of their pagan faith. Our problem as a nation today is not that we are returning to paganism but that we are going beyond it to a more deadly peril—the setting aside of light. We are not returning to paganistic darkness but going on into even more profound darkness. But the courtesy which these people showed is an indication of the work of the Holy Spirit in preparing them to hear the word that Paul preached.

Paul's witness began with the remarkable incident involving the viper. It is noteworthy that the Apostle Paul was gathering sticks along with everyone else in this ship's company. He did not draw himself up and (as some might be inclined to do today) say, "I beg your pardon! I'm a man of the cloth. This kind of work is beneath me. While you work I'll direct the activity."

Paul took up a bundle of sticks in which, unknown to him, was a snake torpid with cold. When he laid the bundle on the fire the snake suddenly came to life and bit him on the hand. Luke describes it very vividly. He says that the snake was dangling from Paul's hand. It is clear that it was a severe bite which punctured the skin and allowed the poison to enter Paul's body.

Theological Explanation

The natives immediately recognized the snake as a poisonous viper. They expected to see Paul soon fall over dead or at least to swell up—the normal results of snakebite. Of course they had a theological explanation for why he was bitten. These were religious people, as all primitive men are, and they believed that calamity is always proof of evil. So they surmised that this man was a murderer; that must be why he was a prisoner. He had escaped from the sea, but justice, in the hands of the invisible fates, had not allowed him to escape. Now it had laid hold of him and he was bound to die. But as they watched and saw no harm coming, they changed their minds and decided that he was a god.

What should we make of this? Why did this incident occur on this occasion? No doubt here we have one of the "signs of an apostle" which Paul refers to in Second Corinthians 12. This links very clearly with the passage at the close of Mark's Gospel, which appears as a footnote in the Revised Standard Version. The Lord Jesus, appearing to his disciples after his resurrection, said to them:

> And these signs will accompany those who believe: in my name they will cast out demons; they will speak in new tongues; *they will pick up serpents,* and if they drink any deadly thing, it will not hurt them; they will lay their hands on the sick, and they will recover (Mark 16:17,18).

In this last chapter of Acts we have two of those signs manifested by the Apostle Paul: he picked up a serpent and it did not harm him, and he laid hands on the sick, as we will see in a moment, and they recovered. Many have misread that passage in Mark and have taken it to mean that this series of miraculous wonders ought to accompany *anyone* who believes in the gospel. But that is to read it without careful recognition of the context. The passage begins with our Lord, risen from the dead, rebuking these disciples because of *their* unbelief, specifically their unbelief in his resurrection. It is a great commentary on the power of unbelief that these men were gathered around with the Lord standing there in front of them and yet some of them were still troubled about the resurrection. Isn't that amazing? The Lord rebuked them because they would not believe the evidence so clearly set before them.

Then he added these words: "These signs will accompany those who believe . . .", i.e., ". . . those among you who believe in my resurrection. . . ." He means this group immediately before him. These signs will accompany *them* as confirmation that they have believed in a risen Lord and will confirm the message that they speak. It was necessary for the apostles to preach the gospel of the Lord Jesus in resurrection power. Therefore it was necessary first that they really believe in his resurrection. And so, our Lord indicated, these signs would confirm it to those among them who believed. Mark concludes the account by saying,

> So then the Lord Jesus, after he had
> spoken to them, was taken up into
> heaven, and sat down at the right hand
> of God. And *they* went forth [who?
> These disciples who heard him] and
> preached everywhere [in obedience to
> the great commission], while the Lord
> worked *with them* and confirmed the
> message by the signs that attended it
> (Mark 16:19,20).

So we have here what Paul calls the signs of an apostle. They established his right and authority to speak to these people, and he demonstrated two of these signs on this occasion. The second is recorded in the next section—the healing of Publius' father:

> Now in the neighborhood of that place
> were lands belonging to the chief man
> of the island, named Publius, who
> received us and entertained us
> hospitably for three days. It happened
> that the father of Publius lay sick with
> fever and dysentery; and Paul visited
> him and prayed, and putting his hands
> on him healed him (Acts 28:7,8).

"They shall lay hands on the sick, and they shall recover." So this again was one of the signs of an apostle which was to accompany those who had seen the risen Lord and who *believed* that he was indeed risen from the dead. It may also be a manifestation of the gift of healing which Paul mentions in First Corinthians 12. It is a clear-cut case of the instantaneous healing of an individual by prayer and the laying on of hands.

Luke tells us that Publius was the "chief man" of the island. That was not merely a description of his standing in society; it was an official title given him as the head of the Roman government on Malta, and the title should perhaps be capitalized: "Chief Man." Publius owned certain lands near where the shipwreck occurred. It is likely that Julius told this Roman governor what kind of man Paul was, and so Publius welcomed the apostle and his party into his home with kindness. Wherever you find kindness demonstrated, the grace of God is always behind it, so Publius also shows evidence that the Spirit had prepared his heart.

While there, Paul learns that Publius' father is ill. Luke, as a physician, diagnoses the case. He says he was sick with fever and dysentery, which sounds very much like the common symptoms of the flu today. So Paul went in to see him and prayed with him. Then he laid his hands on him as an act of identity, and he was instantaneously healed. Notice that this is very similar to the case we read of in Mark's Gospel in which the Lord Jesus went to see Peter and found his mother-in-law sick with fever. And taking her by the hand he raised her up and healed her instantaneously. The healing of Publius' father confirms that Paul is an accredited servant of the same Lord Jesus.

Gradual Cures

In the next section we have a most interesting corollary to this. We read of the healing of many on the island:

> And when this had taken place, the rest
> of the people on the island who had
> diseases also came and were cured.
> They presented many gifts to us; and
> when we sailed, they put on board
> whatever we needed (Acts 28:9,10).

There is a very interesting use of words here.
When Luke says that Publius' father was healed,
he uses a Greek word which means instantaneous
healing. But when he says that these people were
cured, he uses another Greek word which refers
to a more gradual cure. It is an entirely different
word. Not all of them were instantaneously healed.

Therefore many scholars have felt that we
have here a unique combination of medical skill
and divine healing, that Luke was involved as a
physician in these cures which took place during
their three-month stay on the island. There is a
beautiful blending, without any contradiction, of
these two gifts of God: the skill of medicine in
curing, and the divine power of God at work in
direct healing. The two stem from the same wisdom and power of God and can work together
beautifully, as we see in this account. At any
rate, many were cured, and as a result, when they
came to leave, the people gave them, literally,
many "honorariums." The people expressed
their gratitude by stocking the ship with supplies.

Now we read of the remainder of the journey
to Rome:

> After three months we set sail in a ship

which had wintered in the island, a ship
of Alexandria, with the Twin Brothers
as figurehead. Putting in at Syracuse,
we stayed there for three days. And
from there we made a circuit and arrived at Rhegium; and after one day a
south wind sprang up, and on the second day we came to Puteoli. There we
found brethren, and were invited to
stay with them for seven days (Acts
28:11-14a).

With characteristic attention to detail, Luke
gives us a description of the ship. It had as its
figurehead carved images of the Twin Brothers,
Castor and Pollux, the twin sons of Zeus, or
Jupiter. Thus it was obviously a ship dedicated to
a pagan deity. They traveled in this ship from
Malta some eighty miles north to the Island of
Sicily, where they put in at the port of Syracuse.
They stayed there for three days and then sailed
across the Straits of Messina to Rhegium, which
is at the very tip of the toe of the Italian boot.
Then, a south wind blowing them directly north,
they made their way quickly up the coast and
landed at Puteoli, the great port in which all the
ships unloaded as they brought grain from Egypt
to Rome. It was 130 miles from Rome, near the
present city of Naples. There Paul disembarked
and began the final stage of his journey.

Here we get a wonderful note: at Puteoli he
was met by Christians. This is a remarkable
evidence of the spread of Christianity even this
early, probably about A.D. 60. Paul had never
been to Italy before. Nor, to our knowledge, had

any of the other apostles. And yet there were Christians in many of the cities of Italy as well as in Rome itself. Here are some who are waiting to greet Paul when he lands, still 130 miles from Rome.

> And so we came to Rome. And the brethren there, when they heard of us, came as far as the Forum of Appius and Three Taverns to meet us. On seeing them Paul thanked God and took courage. And when we came into Rome, Paul was allowed to stay by himself, with the soldier that guarded him (Acts 28:14b-16).

Rome at last! And two companies of Christians came out from Rome to meet him: one came as far as the Forum of Appius, which was forty miles from Rome; another came thirty miles out to the Three Taverns. If you want to walk in the footsteps of Paul you can go to Rome and walk this same road. The Appian Way is still there, and you can see these very places.

What an event this must have been! And what a delightful note is added by the way the body of believers met Paul and encouraged his heart. As he approached the city he evidently felt some fear and trepidation. He did not know what was going to happen to him when he appeared before Nero. He must have been very uncertain as to whether he would ever again be free from imprisonment. But what a comfort it was that these early Christians eagerly welcomed Paul and prayed with him and strengthened him, thus encouraging his heart as he came at last to Rome. When he arrived in Rome he could see God's hand still at work in the fact that he was given courteous and lenient treatment and was allowed to stay by himself in his own house, with the soldiers who guarded him.

Last Appeal to the Jews

The last major episode of this account occurs now in the final section. In his letter to the Romans Paul said, "I am not ashamed of the gospel: it is the power of God for salvation to everyone who has faith, to the Jew first and also to the Greek." Paul always maintained that it was his responsibility to go to the Jew first and then to the Greek. Here we have the last account in Scripture of that process and priority:

> After three days he called together the local leaders of the Jews; and when they had gathered, he said to them, "Brethren, though I had done nothing against the people or the customs of our fathers, yet I was delivered prisoner from Jerusalem into the hands of the Romans. When they had examined me, they wished to set me at liberty, because there was no reason for the death penalty in my case. But when the Jews objected, I was compelled to appeal to Caesar—though I had no charge to bring against my nation (Acts 28: 17-19).

As Paul had always done, he began with the Jews. He invited the local Jewish leaders to come

and see him. He could not go to them, because he
was bound to a Roman guard. It is interesting
that they responded. They did not know him,
though perhaps they had heard of him. But
because he had been a member of the Sanhedrin,
the Jewish colony was at least willing to listen to
him. He simply explained his predicament,
pointing out that he was an innocent victim of
this strange hostility of the Jews toward him. He
had done nothing against his nation. He himself
was a Jew who longed to bless his people and
help them. But he found them strangely hostile.
Even the Romans, when the Jews turned him
over to them, wanted to let him go because they
could find no cause of death in him. But the Jews
objected. And Paul makes clear that it was the
Jews who were against him, not he against them.
He had no charge to bring against his nation.

How amazing! How gracious is his forgiving
spirit! As we read this book we have seen how
Jewish zealots had hounded him and caused
trouble for him in every city. They had aroused
the populace against him, had beaten and caused
him to be scourged and stoned. But he speaks not
one word of resentment against these people, not
one word of indictment or vindictiveness. He
freely absolves them of any charge.

Because of the Hope

He then points out the real reason why the
Jews so consistently opposed him:

> For this reason therefore I have asked
> to see you and speak with you, *since it
> is because of the hope of Israel* that I

am bound with this chain (Acts 28:20).

He means by that phrase the promised coming of the Messiah. Now, almost two thousand years later, this is still the crucial issue in Israel—the promise of the Messiah. This issue has never been settled and never can be. It remains a constant thorn in the side of any Jewish community. If you want to cause disturbance and arouse argument, to evoke resentment and curiosity, you merely have to raise the issue of the Messiah and you will find the same kind of reaction that Paul experienced. Jews immediately become deeply concerned and involved. Many, as Paul did, are turning to Christ these days, as they re-examine this question. Now we get the response:

> And they said to him, "We have receiv-
> ed no letters from Judea about you,
> and none of the brethren coming here
> has reported or spoken any evil about
> you. But we desire to hear from you
> what your views are; for with regard to
> this sect we know that everywhere it is
> spoken against" (Acts 28:21,22).

It is rather revealing that these Jews in Rome had received no word about the apostle. It is possible, of course, that they could not have received word before this any more than Paul could have reached Rome before this. The news may have been delayed. But it is much more likely that the Jews in Jerusalem had given up trying to trap Paul by legal means, by Roman authority. And perhaps the reason he was detained as a prisoner in Rome for two more years was that the Romans were waiting for some kind of accusation to come from Jerusalem. This situation left his case undecided—no one knew what to do. But the Jews in Rome were eager to hear his views. Their curiosity had been aroused because they had heard that this strange sect which had gathered around Jesus of Nazareth was spoken against everywhere in the Jewish communities. So they appointed a day:

> When they had appointed a day for him, they came to him at his lodging in great numbers. And he expounded the matter to them from morning till evening, testifying to the kingdom of God and trying to convince them about Jesus both from the law of Moses and from the prophets (Acts 28:23).

What a magnificent Bible study this must have been! What an opportunity these Jews in Rome had as this mighty apostle began to go systematically through the Scriptures. Obviously their curiosity was greatly aroused and they gathered in large numbers. They set aside an ample period of time, taking the whole day from morning till evening to debate and discuss and examine the Scriptures. And they certainly had a competent teacher. Who could have interpreted these Old Testament passages better or known them more thoroughly than this former Pharisee, trained as a scholar, who knew the Old Testament almost by heart?

And they had a most fascinating subject— Jesus in the Old Testament. Paul spoke to them about the kingdom of God, that is, God's rule over all the earth, and about Jesus, the way to the heart of God. He tried desperately, by patiently expounding to them many of the great passages in the law and the prophets, to convince them that Jesus was indeed the Messiah.

Nothing is more fascinating than to see how these amazing predictions of the Old Testament focus upon one Person in all of history and upon the events of his 33½ years of life on earth. He is the fulfillment of prophecies stretched over hundreds and hundreds of years of previous history. The writings of the prophets center around this one brief moment in history when a Man should be born in Bethlehem, live in Nazareth, tread the hills of Judea, do mighty works, and finally die on a cross as predicted, but then be raised again from the dead exactly as predicted.

Discouraging Results

We can guess some of the passages Paul must have used on this occasion. How vivid and clear they are! How many people yet today are still arrested by the accuracy of these great Old Testament predictions! What tremendous, compelling proof he set before these people. And yet . . . look at the discouraging results:

> And some were convinced by what he said, while others disbelieved. So, as they disagreed among themselves, they departed, after Paul had made one statement: "The Holy Spirit was right in saying to your fathers through Isaiah the prophet:

'Go to this people, and say,
you shall indeed hear but never understand,
and you shall indeed see but never
perceive' " (Acts 28:24-26).

Why? The passage goes on to tell us why:

" 'For this people's heart has
grown dull,
and their ears are heavy of hearing,
and their eyes they have closed;
lest they should perceive with their
eyes, and hear with their ears,
and understand with their heart,
and turn for me to heal them' "
(Acts 28:27).

The perversity of human nature! This passage
predicts that people would deliberately close
their minds because they did not want to hear the
ultimate message. Many of us have done this. We
have anticipated, at the gut level, where it was all
going to come out, and it has been different than
what we have wanted, and so we have shut our
ears and eyes and minds, and have not listened.
And Paul says that is what happened here, as
Isaiah had predicted. The amazing thing is that
he uses this passage from Isaiah in exactly the
same way that Jesus himself had used it in his last
encounter with the Jews. In the twelfth chapter
of John's Gospel we read:

When Jesus had said this, he departed
and hid himself from them. Though he
had done so many signs before them,
yet they did not believe in him; it was

that the word spoken by the prophet Isaiah might be fulfilled:

"Lord, who has believed our report, and to whom has the arm of the Lord been revealed?"

Therefore they could not believe. For Isaiah again said,

"He has blinded their eyes and hardened their heart, lest they should see with their eyes and receive with their heart, and turn for me to heal them" (John 12:36-40).

And then John adds this amazing word:

Isaiah said this because he saw his glory and spoke of him [i.e., of Jesus] (John 12:41).

And if we read the sixth chapter of Isaiah, from which that quotation comes, we find that itis the passage in which Isaiah said,

In the year that King Uzziah died I saw the Lord sitting upon a throne, high and lifted up; and his train filled the temple. Above him stood the seraphim. . . . And one called to another and said:

"Holy, holy, holy is the Lord of hosts;
the whole earth is full of his glory" (Isaiah 6:1-3).

Thus John says that Isaiah saw Jesus ana beheld his glory and spoke of him. And yet Paul must say to these Jewish leaders:

Let it be known to you then that this

salvation of God has been sent to the
Gentiles; they will listen (Acts 28:28).

With sad hearts the apostle and his friends saw
these Jews turn away once again. This is the last
time in Scripture in which you find the appeal of
the gospel officially set before the Jewish people.
One of the great mysteries of all time is Jewish
unbelief. How can this people miss these tremendous passages, this clear-cut delineation of their
Messiah? And yet what happened here as recorded in this passage is nothing other than what is
happening in much of the church today. What
was the reason these people refused to move? As
you analyze the account you can see that it was
because it meant change. They had worked out a
comfortable theological explanation of who the
Messiah would be. When God moved in ways
different from what they had expected, even
though he had predicted it, they refused to move
with him. They hung back and clung to their
tradition and refused to be disturbed in the comfort of their lives. They did not want to be
changed.

And that is the problem today. Many Christians are doing the same thing. Having mis-
understood much of Scripture and applied it in
ways that are not warranted, and having
developed a very comfortable pattern of
life—when the Spirit of God moves in fresh and
vital ways, we do not want to change and will not
follow. We resist anything that disturbs the tran-
quility of an accepted and commonly practiced
tradition. We want to cling to the comfortable

dead rags of the past even though the Word of God has always marked out the pathway by which the Spirit works. What a lesson this ought to be to us! As God bypassed the Jews, so he bypasses any who continually refuse to move with the creative power of the Spirit of God.

And so we come to the last two verses:

> And he lived there two whole years at his own expense, and welcomed all who came to him, preaching the kingdom of God and teaching about the Lord Jesus Christ quite openly and unhindered (Acts 28:30,31).

This is what I like to call the end of the beginning. The Book of Acts is just the beginning of the record of the operaton of the body of Christ at work in the world since his resurrection and ascension. It is just the first chapter. We have come now to the last page of that chapter. The rest of the record is being written as history unfolds. Fresh and wonderful chapters are now being written in our own day, ultimately to be incorporated into this account. It is a tremendous privilege and joy to be a part of this divine record.

The Gospel Unhindered

One of the most impressive things about this last section is the last word. Do you notice how the Book of Acts ends? With the word "unhindered." That word describes the freedom of the gospel. You see, *Paul* was hindered. He could not go about the city. He was still chained day and night to a Roman guard. But he could welcome friends in. And he could walk around his house and yard and he could minister and teach there. Paul never chafed under this restraint. His letters from this period are filled with joy and rejoicing. He never fretted about his condition, but instead welcomed all who came, and sent letters back with them—letters that have changed the world. It was during this time that Paul wrote Philippians, Ephesians, Colossians, and the letter to Philemon. What tremendous truths are set forth in these letters which he had time to write because he could no longer travel abroad! You and I can be grateful that God kept Paul still long enough to write them; otherwise we might have been deprived of these great messages which have changed the history of man time and time again.

Still, Paul had yet to appear before the emperor. In the next year or so a great persecution broke out under the vicious emperor Nero, one of the greatest persecutions that Christians have ever experienced. But the Word was not hindered. No matter what the condition of the church, the Word of God is never bound. We must remember that.

Tradition and other Scripture suggest to us that at the end of this two-year period, which brings us up to the time Luke wrote this book, the apostle was released. Apparently he did appear before the Emperor and his case was dismissed. He went back to the Island of Crete, where he left Titus in charge, as the letter to Titus tells us. And he probably visited Ephesus once again, even though he had said to them as he left, "You'll never see my face again." It is very likely that Paul did come back, and that he left Timothy in charge there. It is also very likely that he went to Spain, as he hungered to do. And some scholars feel that Paul may even have visited Britain and preached there.

In any case, it is clear that Paul was eventually arrested again. This time, instead of being allowed to live in a hired home, he was thrown into that dark and slimy dungeon called the Mammertime Prison, which you can still visit in Rome. There he wrote his second letter to Timothy, which reflects the conditions of that confinement—cold and dank, lonely and isolated. And finally, according to tradition, Paul was led out one day in the early spring and taken outside the walls of Rome. There he knelt down and a sword flashed in the sun. His head was cut off and the apostle went home to be with the Lord.

If we will be obedient to what is set forth in such clear language in the Book of Acts, God will supply all the power and vitality we need. And the sweeping changes made possible by the life of Christ in his body can occur among us today just as they occurred in that first century. The principles by which the church is to operate are declared here. The power available to us is exactly the same. The conditions of the world in which we live are exactly the same. Therefore nothing needs to be changed in the record of the Book of Acts. The life of the body of Christ is to go on in this twentieth century exactly as it was lived in the first. May God grant that we will be men and women of faith, with vigor and vision, willing to move with the creative, innovative Spirit in our day and age, so that we might share in the triumphs of the gospel.